CATS
AND THE LAW

By Anmarie Barrie, Esq.

CATS
AND THE LAW

BY ANMARIE BARRIE, ESQ.

Humorous drawings by Andrew Prendimano. Illustrative art by John R. Quinn, Scott Boldt and P.D. Protsenko.

CONTENTS

CONTENTS

© Copyright 1990 by T.F.H. Publications, Inc.

Distributed in the UNITED STATES by T.F.H. Publications, Inc., One T.F.H. Plaza, Neptune City, NJ 07753; in CANADA to the Pet Trade by H & L Pet Supplies Inc., 27 Kingston Crescent, Kitchener, Ontario N2B 2T6; Rolf C. Hagen Ltd., 3225 Sartelon Street, Montreal 382 Quebec; in CANADA to the Book Trade by Macmillan of Canada (A Division of Canada Publishing Corporation), 164 Commander Boulevard, Agincourt, Ontario M1S 3C7; in ENGLAND by T.F.H. Publications Limited, Cliveden House/Priors Way/Bray, Maidenhead, Berkshire SL6 2HP, England; in AUSTRALIA AND THE SOUTH PACIFIC by T.F.H. (Australia) Pty. Ltd., Box 149, Brookvale 2100 N.S.W., Australia; in NEW ZEALAND by Ross Haines & Son, Ltd., 82 D Elizabeth Knox Place, Panmure, Auckland, New Zealand; in the PHILIPPINES by Bio-Research, 5 Lippay Street, San Lorenzo Village, Makati Rizal; in SOUTH AFRICA by Multipet Pty. Ltd., Box 235 New Germany, South Africa 3620. Published by T.F.H. Publications, Inc. Manufactured in the United States of America by T.F.H. Publications, Inc.

The responsible cat owner will familiarize himself with his municipality's laws regarding cats.

CAVEAT

This book is written merely as a general survey of the laws pertaining to cats. The laws vary tremendously from jurisdiction to jurisdiction. They also change over time, and are subject to the interpretation of the controlling authorities.

Any reference to a resource material or facility is not an endorsement.

The author, Anmarie Barrie, Esq., is a graduate of Seton Hall School of Law in Newark, New Jersey. She holds the degrees of Bachelor of Science in dental hygiene and Master of Business Administration. She has written more than a dozen books on pet animals, including *Dogs and the Law*.

Cats are among the most popular of domestic pets.

Cats As Pets

It is impossible to say which pet is the most numerous in the world. Cats, though, are surely among the most popular. Each year the number of cats kept as pets increases. The cat has become the pet of choice for many urban dwellers. In fact, some experts believe that cats outnumber dogs as pets in the United States and some other Western countries.

Cats are the only domestic pet which live a solitary life in the wild. This independent lifestyle is the reason cats are regarded by many humans as antisocial. Yet it is also because of this independence and aloofness that millions of people consider the cat the ultimate pet. A cat is easy to keep: it is clean; it does not need to be walked or bathed; it can be housebroken; and it is content to be alone all day whether it is indoors or out. Since a cat does not require a lot of attention or a lot of space, it is a perfect pet for people who live in apartments or who have busy schedules. Additionally, cats exhibit a wide range of personalities which add to their delightfulness as pets.

Basically, a cat merely requires sound nutrition, minimal grooming, and a place to sleep. Other than that, a cat takes care of itself. It has an extraordinary ability to survive in a range of environments. A cat is an intelligent animal which quickly learns things that are to its advantage, such as opening cupboard doors.

Most kittens become affectionate and friendly if they are handled a lot when they are two to seven weeks old. They will allow their owner to pick them up, cuddle, and stroke them. A cat which lacks human interaction when it is young may remain shy all its life.

Disciplining a cat requires time, patience, and consistency on your part.

With further persistence, a cat may be trained to respond to its name and to other commands. Due to its social make-up, though, and not because of any lack of intelligence, a cat cannot be trained to the same extent as a dog. Whereas a dog accepts discipline from an authority figure, a cat does not take kindly to instruction. A dog is a pack animal whose survival depends on its ability to live in a community. A cat instinctively behaves only in terms of what is best for its own well-being.

Cats have been bred and raised in the home for thousands of years.

DOMESTICATION

It is not known exactly when humans first associated with cats. The earliest record of felines within human camps dates back to around 7500 B.C. in Jericho. Not until settlements grew larger, though, did cats become obvious. It can be reasonably supposed that cats were commonplace by about 2500 B.C. in and around biblical lands. However, there is no evidence that cats were being selectively bred or kept within the home at this time.

11

CATS AND THE LAW

The establishment of a cat cult in Egypt around 1500 B.C. underscores the fact that cats were kept in homes and were considered sacred. Cats were mummified and some gods took the form of cats. Injuring a cat was a serious offense. During this period, the Egyptians, Assyrians, and other peoples developed considerable cat breeding skills. Cats are believed to have been common in Indian households from as early as 2000 B.C., and in Chinese homes from about 1000 B.C. Cats were kept in Turkey by about 600 B.C.

Tameness should not be confused with domestication. The fact that an animal may be kept and even bred within a captive human environment does not make it a domesticated species; any wild animal can be tamed to some extent. Domestication is reached only when a wild species is selectively bred to the degree that physical, anatomical, and behavioral changes render the animal incapable of surviving if it were returned to the wild. Many animals, such as the dog, are fully domesticated.

Cats, however, are the most wild and independent of all domestic animals. The extent of domestication is so relatively low in many cat breeds that the majority of them would have little difficulty in returning to their wild habitat. Even a housecat retains efficient killing and hunting instincts.

In the wild, a cat lives in relative isolation. The cat evolved to live alone, hunt alone, and to fight its own battles. It has no dependence on its own kind other than to reproduce. This independent nature of the cat makes domestication a slow process—which the cat is still undergoing. A cat may appear domesticated on the outside, but it still has a wild nature. Hence, the cat holds a unique place among domestic pets.

Much of the unsociability of a cat is removed if there is an adequate food supply. Therefore, in a domestic environment, a cat will display new patterns in its social organization. A cat can form a strong bond with a person or even another animal.

CATS AND SOCIETY

As civilization advances and living conditions become more crowded, laws are created to keep society functioning smoothly. Our lives become more regulated, and this includes how we care for our cats.

Laws dealing with cats are found at the federal, state and municipal levels of government. Mostly, though, cat law is a local affair. There are so many laws, and they vary so much from region to region, that it would be impractical to address them all in this book. However, there are general rules and guidelines that can be discussed. This book will teach you how to research and utilize the laws relevant to your particular area.

Even the most tame household cat retains its instinct to hunt and kill.

Your local public library can be a good source of information regarding simple legal questions.

Legal Research

Legal research can be as easy as going to your public library, law school library, or public courthouse library. For federal laws, read the United States Constitution, federal statutes (laws passed by Congress), and federal case law (decisions rendered by the federal courts).

For state law, refer to your State Constitution, state law (laws passed by the state legislature), and state case law (decisions rendered by the state court). Finding out about city ordinances (laws enacted by the city council and county boards) is usually as simple as opening a three-ring binder and reading the entries under "Cats." These municipal codes are often found at the city clerk's or city attorney's office. Sometimes a simple legal question can be answered by the humane society, animal control center, department of health, or local pet shop.

When looking for a statute, ordinance, or case, it should be easy to find if you have a citation (a reference). Usually, laws are merely numbered and listed in order. For example, Ky. Rev. Stat. §258.275 refers to the reference work entitled Kentucky Revised Statutes, section 258.275. Since the title of state statute books are abbreviated in a citation, the abbreviations and full titles of state code books are presented here.

California, New York, Texas, and Maryland arrange their statutes into subject codes, such as Civil, Education, Penal, etc. Then the subject codes are arranged numerically. For example, Cal. Civ. Code §3342, refers to the California Civil Code, section 3342. A list of the subject codes of these four states, and their abbreviations, is listed below.

A case citation may look like this:

Henkel v. Jordan, 7 Kan.App.2d 561, 644 P.2d 1348, 30 A.L.R.4th 978 (1982).

(Text continues on page 24)

State Code Books

Abbreviation	*Full Title*
Ala. Code	Code of Alabama
Alaska Stat.	Alaska Statutes
Ann. Mis. Stat.	Annotated Missouri Statutes
Ariz. Rev. Stat. Ann.	Arizona Revised Statutes Annotated
Ark. Stat. Ann.	Arkansas Statutes Annotated
Cal. (subject) Code	Annotated California Code
Colo. Rev. Stat. Ann.	Colorado Revised Statutes Annotated
Conn. Gen. Stat.	General Statutes of Connecticut
Conn. Gen. Stat. Ann.	Connecticut General Statutes Annotated
Cons. Law of N.Y.	Consolidated Law of N.Y.
D.C. Code Ann.	District of Columbia Code Annotated
D.C. Code Encycl.	District of Columbia Code Encyclopedia
Del. Code Ann.	Delaware Code Annotated
Fla. Stat.	Florida Statutes
Fla. Stat. Ann.	Florida Statutes Annotated
Ga. Code Ann.	Code of Georgia Annotated
Hawaii Rev. Stat.	Hawaii Revised Statutes
Idaho Code	Idaho Code
Ill. Rev. Stat.	Illinois Revised Statutes
Ill. Ann. Stat.	Illinois Annotated Statutes
Ind. Code	Indiana Code
Ind. Code Ann.	Annotated Indiana Code or Indiana Statutes Annotated Code
Iowa Code	Code of Iowa
Iowa Code Ann.	Iowa Code Annotated
Kan. Stat. Ann.	Kansas Statutes Annotated
Ky. Rev. Stat.	Kentucky Revised Statutes
Ky. Rev. Stat. Ann.	Kentucky Revised Statutes Annotated
La. Rev. Stat. Ann.	Louisiana Revised Statutes Annotated

La. Civ. Code Ann.	Louisiana Civil Code Annotated
L.S.A.	Louisiana Civil Code
Mass. Gen. Laws Ann.	Massachusetts General Laws Annotated
Mass. Ann. Laws	Annotated Laws of Massachusetts
Md. (subject) Code Ann.	Annotated Code of Maryland
Md. Ann. Code	Maryland Annotated Code
Me. Rev. Stat. Ann.	Maine Revised Statutes Annotated
Mich. Comp. Laws	Michigan Compiled Laws
Mich. Comp. Laws Ann.	Michigan Compiled Laws Annotated
Mich. Stat. Ann.	Michigan Statutes Annotated
Minn. Stat.	Minnesota Statutes
Minn. Stat. Ann.	Minnesota Statutes Annotated
Miss. Code	Mississippi Code
Miss. Code Ann.	Mississippi Code Annotated
Mo. Ann. Stat.	Annotated Missouri Statutes
Mont. Code Ann.	Montana Code Annotated
Mo. Rev. Stat.	Missouri Revised Statutes
N.C. Gen. Stat. Ann.	General Statutes of North Carolina Annotated
N.D. Cent. Code Ann.	North Dakota Century Code Annotated
Neb. Rev. Stat.	Revised Statutes of Nebraska
Nev. Rev. Stat. Ann.	Nevada Revised Statutes Annotated
N.H. Rev. Stat. Ann.	New Hampshire Revised Statutes Annotated
N.J.S.A.	New Jersey Statutes Annotated
N.J. Stat. Ann.	New Jersey Statutes Annotated
N.M. Stat. Ann.	New Mexico Statutes Annotated
N.Y. (subject) Law	Consolidated Laws of New York Annotated
Ohio Rev. Code Ann.	Ohio Revised Code Annotated
Okla. Stat.	Oklahoma Statutes
Okla. Stat. Ann.	Oklahoma Statutes Annotated
Ore. Rev. Stat.	Oregon Revised Statutes
Pa. Cons. Stat.	Pennsylvania Consolidated Statutes
Pa. Cons. Stat. Ann.	Pennsylvania Consolidated Statutes Annotated

Pa. Stat. Ann.	Pennsylvania Statutes Annotated
P.R. Laws Ann.	Puerto Rico Laws Annotated
R.I. Gen. Laws Ann.	General Laws of Rhode Island Annotated
S.C. Code Ann.	Code of Laws of South Carolina Annotated
S.D. Codified Laws Ann.	South Dakota Codified Laws Annotated
S.D. Comp. Laws Ann.	South Dakota Compiled Laws Annotated
South Dak. Codif. Laws	South Dakota Codified Laws
Tenn. Code Ann.	Tennessee Code Annotated
Tex. (subject) Code Ann.	Texas Codes Annotated
Tex. Stat. Ann.	Texas Statutes Annotated
Tex. Rev. Civ. Stat. Ann.	Texas Revised Civil Statutes Annotated
U.S.C.	United States Code
U.S.C.A.	United States Code Annotated
U.S.C.S.	United States Code Service
Utah Code Ann.	Utah Code Annotated
Va. Code	Code of Virginia Annotated
Vt. Stat. Ann.	Vermont Statutes Annotated
Wash. Rev. Code	Revised Code of Washington
Wash. Rev. Code Ann.	Revised Code of Washington Annotated
Wis. Stat.	Wisconsin Statutes
Wis. Stat. Ann.	Wisconsin Statutes Annotated
W.Va. Code Ann.	West Virginia Code Annotated
Wyom. Stat. Ann.	Wyoming Statutes Annotated

State Subject Codes

Abbreviation	Subject Code
California	
Agric.	Agricultural
Bus. & Prof.	Business and Professions
Civ.	Civil
Civ. Proc.	Civil Procedure
Com.	Commercial
Corp.	Corporations
Educ.	Education
Elec.	Elections
Evid.	Evidence
Fin.	Financial
Fish & Game	Fish and Game
Food & Agric.	Food and Agricultural
Gov.	Government
Harb. & Nav.	Harbors and Navigation
Health & Safety	Health and Safety
Ins.	Insurance
Lab.	Labor
Mil. & Vet.	Military and Veterans
Penal	Penal
Prob.	Probate
Pub. Con.	Public Contract
Pub. Res.	Public Resources
Pub. Util.	Public Utilities
Rev. & T.	Revenue and Taxation
Str. & H.	Streets and Highways
Un. Ins.	Unemployment Insurance
Veh.	Vehicle
Water	Water
Welf. & Inst.	Welfare and Institutions

Maryland

Com. Law	Commercial Law
Const.	Constitutions
Corps. & Ass'ns	Corporations and Associations
Cts. & Jud. Proc.	Courts and Judicial Proceedings
Educ.	Education
Env.	Environmental
Est. & Trusts	Estates and Trusts
Fam. Law	Family Law
Fin. Inst.	Financial Institutions
Health Env.	Health—Environmental
Health Gen.	Health—General
Health Occ.	Health Occupations
Nat. Res.	Natural Resources
Real Prop.	Real Property
St. Fin. & Proc.	State Finance and Procurement
State Gov't	State Government
Tax Gen.	Tax—General
Transp.	Transportation

New York

Aband. Prop.	Abandoned Property
Agric. Conserv. & Adj.	Agricultural Conservation and Adjustment
Agric. & Mkts.	Agriculture and Markets
Alco. Bev. Cont.	Alcoholic Beverage Control
Alt. County Gov't	Alternative County Government
Arts & Cult. Aff.	Arts and Cultural Affairs
Banking	Banking
Ben. Ord.	Benevolent Orders
Bus. Corp.	Business Corporation
Canal	Canal
Civ. Prac. Law & R.	Civil Practice Law and Rules
Civ. Rights	Civil Rights
Civ. Serv.	Civil Service
Com.	Commerce
Condem.	Condemnation
Const.	Constitution
Coop. Corp.	Cooperative Corporations

Correct.	Corrections
County	County
Crim. Proc.	Criminal Procedure
Debt. & Cred.	Debtor and Creditor
Dom. Rel.	Domestic Relations
Econ. Dev.	Economic Development
Educ.	Education
Elec.	Election
Em. Dom. Proc.	Eminent Domain Procedure
Empl'rs Liab.	Employers' Liability
Energy	Energy
Envtl. Conserv.	Environmental Conservation
Est. Powers & Trust	Estates, Powers, and Trusts
Exec.	Executive
Gen. Ass'ns	General Associations
Gen. Bus.	General Business
Gen. City	General City
Gen. Constr.	General Construction
Gen. Mun.	General Municipal
Gen. Oblig.	General Obligations
High.	Highway
Indian	Judiciary—Court Acts
Ins.	Indian
Jud.	Insurance
Jud. Ct. Acts	Judiciary
Lab.	Labor
Legis.	Legislative
Lien	Lien
Local Fin.	Local Finance
Mental Hyg.	Mental Hygiene
Mil.	Military
Mult. Dwell.	Multiple Dwelling
Mult. Resid.	Multiple Residence
Mun. Home Rule	Municipal Home Rule
Nav.	Navigation
Not-For-Profit Corp.	Not-For-Profit Corporation
Opt. County Gov.	Optional County Government
PRHPL	Parks, Recreation, and Historical Preservation
Partnership	Partnership

Penal	Penal
Pers. Prop.	Personal Property
Priv. Hous. Fin.	Private Housing Finance
Pub. Auth.	Public Authorities
Pub. Bldgs.	Public Buildings
Pub. Health	Public Health
Pub. Hous.	Public Housing
Pub. Lands	Public Lands
Pub. Off.	Public Officers
Pub. Serv.	Public Service
RPWB	Racing, Pari-Mutuel Wagering, and Breeding
Rapid Trans.	Rapid Transit
Real Prop.	Real Property
RPAPL	Real Property Actions and Proceedings
Real Prop. Tax	Real Property Tax
Relig. Corp.	Religious Corporations
Retire. & Soc. Sec.	Retirement and Social Security
R.R.	Railroad
Rural Elec. Coop.	Rural Electric Cooperative
Salt Springs	Salt Springs
Second Class Cities	Second Class Cities
Soc. Serv.	Social Service
Soil Conserv. Dist.	Soil Conservation Districts
State	State
St. Adm. Proc. Act	State Administrative Procedure Act
State Fin.	State Finance
State Print. & Pub. Doc.	State Printing and Public Documents
Stat. Local Gov'ts	Statute of Local Governments
Surr. Ct. Proc. Act	Surrogate's Court Procedure Act
Tax	Tax
Town	Town
Transp.	Transportation
Transp. Corp.	Transportations Corporations
U.C.C.	Uniform Commercial Code
Uncons. Laws	Unconsolidated Laws
Veh. & Traf.	Vehicle and Traffic
Village	Village
Vol. Fire. Ben.	Volunteer Firemen's Benefit

Work. Comp.	Workmen's Compensation

Texas

Agric.	Agriculture
Alco. Bev.	Alcoholic Beverage
Bus. & Com.	Business and Commerce
Civ. Prac. & Rem.	Civil Practice and Remedies
Corp. & Ass'ns	Corporations and Associations
Crim. Proc.	Criminal Procedure
Educ.	Education
Elec.	Election
Fam.	Family
Fin.	Financial
Gov.	Government
Health & Safety	Health and Safety
High.	Highway
Hum. Res.	Human Resources
Ins.	Insurance
Lab.	Labor
Loc. Gov.	Local Government
Nat. Res.	Natural Resources
Occ.	Occupations
Parks & Wild.	Parks and Wildlife
Penal	Penal
Prob.	Probate
Prop.	Property
Res.	Resources
Tax	Tax
Util.	Utilities
Veh.	Vehicles
Water	Water
Welf.	Welfare

Do not be intimidated. Even though this citation may seem complex at first glance, it is really quite simple. Henkel v. Jordan is the title of the case. Typically, the title names the parties involved in the dispute. In this case, Henkel is the plaintiff and Jordan is the defendant.

Three cites are listed, which means that the case is published in three reference works. Kan.App.2d is the abbreviation for the second edition of the books named the Kansas Court of Appeals Reports. The case is found in volume 7, beginning at page 561. P.2d is the short form of the Pacific Reporter, second edition. The case is printed in volume 644, beginning at page 1348. The third reference book that contains the case is the A.L.R.4th, or the fourth edition of the American Law Reports. Look on page 978 in volume 30. The case was decided in 1982.

You do not have to read the case in all three works. A citation merely lists all the reference books that contain the case as a matter of convenience; not all reference works are found in one library.

Case citations always abbreviate the title of the reference work. Therefore, shown here is a list of abbreviations of the case books you are most likely to encounter in your research. Next to the abbreviation is the full title of the reference work.

Common Legal Abbrevations
and Their Full Titles

Abbreviation	*Full Title*
A., A.2d	Atlantic Reporter
Ala.	Alabama Reports
Ala. App.	Alabama Appellate Court Reports
Alaska	Alaska Reports
Ariz.	Arizona Reports
Ariz. App.	Arizona Appeals Reports
Ark.	Arkansas Reports
Cal., Cal.2d, Cal.3d	California Reports
Cal. Rptr.	West's California Reporter
C.F.R.	Code of Federal Regulations
Colo.	Colorado Reports
Colo. App.	Colorado Court of Appeals Reports
Conn.	Connecticut Reports
Conn. Supp.	Connecticut Supplement
Del.	Delaware Reports
F., F.2d	Federal Reporter
Fed. Reg.	Federal Register
Fla.	Florida Reports
Fla. Supp.	Florida Supplement
F. Supp.	Federal Supplement
Ga.	Georgia Reports
Ga. App.	Georgia Appeals Reports
Hawaii	Hawaii Reports
Idaho	Idaho Reports
Ill., Ill.2d	Illinois Reports
Ill. App., Ill. App.2d	Illinois Appellate Court Reports

Ind.	Indiana Reports
Ind. App.	Indiana Court of Appeals Reports
Iowa	Iowa Reports
Kan.	Kansas Reports
Kan. App., Kan. App.2d	Kansas Court of Appeals Reports
Ky.	Kentucky Reports
La.	Louisiana Reports
Mass.	Massachusetts Reports
Mass. App. Ct.	Massachusetts Appeals Court Reports
Mass. App. Dec.	Appellate Decisions
Me.	Maine Reports
Md.	Maryland Reports
Md. App.	Maryland Appellate Reports
Mich.	Michigan Reports
Mich. App.	Michigan Appeals Reports
Minn.	Minnesota Reports
Miss.	Mississippi Reports
Mo.	Missouri Reports
Mo. App.	Missouri Appeals Reports
Mont.	Montana Reports
N.C.	North Carolina Reports
N.C. Ct. App.	North Carolina Court of Appeals Reports
N.D.	North Dakota Reports
N.E., N.E.2d	North Eastern Reporter
Neb.	Nebraska Reports
Nev.	Nevada Reports
N.H.	New Hampshire Reports
N.J.	New Jersey Reports
N.J. Super.	New Jersey Superior Court Reports
N.M.	New Mexico Reports
N.W., N.W.2d	North Western Reporter
N.Y., N.Y.2d	New York Reports
N.Y.S., N.Y.S.2d	West's New York Supplement
Ohio App., Ohio App.2d	Ohio Appellate Reports
Ohio Misc.	Ohio Miscellaneous
Ohio St., Ohio St.2d	Ohio State Reports
Okla.	Oklahoma Reports

Or.	Oregon Reports
Or. App.	Oregon Reports, Court of Appeals
P., P.2d	Pacific Reporter
Pa.	Pennsylvania State Reports
P.R.	Puerto Rico Reports
P.R. Dec.	Decisiones de Puerto Rico
R.I.	Rhode Island Reports
S.C.	South Carolina Reports
S. Ct.	Supreme Court Reporter
S.D.	South Dakota Reports
S.E., S.E.2d	South Eastern Reporter
So., So.2d	Southern Reporter
S.W., S.W.2d	South Western Reporter
Tenn.	Tennessee Reports
Tenn. App.	Tennessee Appeals
Tex.	Texas Reports
Treas. Reg.	Treasury Regulations
U.S.	United States Reports
U.S. App. D.C.	United States Court of Appeals Reports
U.S.C.	United States Code
U.S.C.A.	United States Code Annotated
U.S.L.W.	United States Law Week
Utah	Utah Reports
Vt.	Vermont Reports
Va.	Virginia Reports
Wash., Wash.2d	Washington Reports
Wash. App.	Washington Appellate Reports
W. Va.	West Virginia Reports
Wis., Wis.2d	Wisconsin Reports
Wyo.	Wyoming Reports

THE NATIONAL REPORTER SYSTEM

The National Reporter System publishes reported decisions of all the states. Each state is not listed in its own volume, however. Rather, the states are split into seven divisions. For each division of states, there is a set of volumes, called a reporter, containing the case law of all those states. Listed below are the seven National Reporters and the states contained within them.

Atlantic Reporter   (A., A2d)
Connecticut
Delaware
District of Columbia
Maine
Maryland
New Hampshire
New Jersey
Pennsylvania
Rhode Island
Vermont

North Eastern Reporter   (N.E., N.E.2d)
Illinois
Indiana
Massachusetts
New York
Ohio

North Western Reporter (N.W., N.W.2d)
Iowa
Michigan
Minnesota
Nebraska
North Dakota
South Dakota
Wisconsin

Pacific Reporter   (P., P.2d)
  Alaska
  Arizona
  California
  Colorado
  Hawaii
  Idaho
  Kansas
  Montana
  Nevada
  New Mexico
  Oklahoma
  Oregon
  Utah
  Washington
  Wyoming

South Eastern Reporter   (S.E., S.E.2d)
  Georgia
  North Carolina
  South Carolina
  Virginia
  West Virginia

Southern Reporter   (So., So.2d)
  Alabama
  Florida
  Louisiana
  Mississippi

South Western Reporter   (S.W., S.W.2d)
  Arkansas
  Kentucky
  Missouri
  Tennesee
  Texas

STATE REPORTS

Most states used to publish a series of books, called reports, that contained court decisions only of their state. Many states, though, have abandoned such a practice and are listed only in the National Reporter System. The states that currently publish their own reports are cited below. All states, whether or not they have their own reference work, are included in the National Reporter system.

State	Full Title of Reference	Abbreviation
Alabama	Alabama Reports	Ala.
	Alabama Appellate Court Reports	Ala. App.
Alaska	Alaska Reports	Alaska
Arizona	Arizona Reports	Ariz.
Arkansas	Arkansas Reports	Ark.
California	California Reports	Cal., Cal.2d, Cal.3d
	California Appellate Reports	Cal.App., Cal.App.2d, Cal.App.3d
	West's California Reporter	Cal.Rptr.
Colorado	Colorado Reports	Colo.
	Colorado Court of Appeals Reports	Colo.App.
Connecticut	Connecticut Reports	Conn.
	Connecticut Supplement	Conn.Supp.
Delaware	Delaware Reports	Del.
Florida	Florida Reports	Fla.
	Florida Supplement	Fla.Supp.
Georgia	Georgia Reports	Ga.
	Georgia Appeals Reports	Ga.App.
Hawaii	Hawaii Reports	Hawaii
Idaho	Idaho Reports	Idaho
Illinois	Illinois Reports	Ill., Ill.2d
	Illinois Appellate Court Reports	Ill.App., Ill.App.2d, Ill.App.3d

Indiana	Indiana Reports	Ind.
	Indiana Court of Appeals Reports	Ind.App.
Iowa	Iowa Reports	Iowa
Kansas	Kansas Reports	Kan.
	Kansas Court of Appeals Reports	Kan.App.
Kentucky	Kentucky Reports	Ky.
Louisiana	Louisiana Reports	La.
Maine	Maine Reports	Me.
Maryland	Maryland Reports	Md.
	Maryland Appellate Reports	Md.App.
Massachusetts	Massachusetts Reports	Mass.
	Massachusetts Appeals Court Reports	Mass.App.Ct.
	Appellate Decisions	Mass.App.Dec.
Michigan	Michigan Reports	Mich.
Minnesota	Minnesota Reports	Minn.
Mississippi	Mississippi Reports	Miss.
Missouri	Missouri Reports	Mo.
	Missouri Appeal Reports	Mo.App.
Montana	Montana Reports	Mont.
Nebraska	Nebraska Reports	Neb.
Nevada	Nevada Reports	Nev.
New Hampshire	New Hampshire Reports	N.H.
New Jersey	New Jersey Reports	N.J.
	New Jersey Superior Court Reports	N.J.Super.
New Mexico	New Mexico Reports	N.M.
New York	New York Reports	N.Y., N.Y.2d
	West's New York Supplement	N.Y.S., N.Y.S.2d
	Appellate Division Reports	A.D., A.D.2d
	New York Miscellaneous Reports	Misc., Misc.2d

North Carolina	North Carolina Reports	N.C.
	North Carolina Court of Appeals Reports	N.C.App.
North Dakota	North Dakota Reports	N.D.
Ohio	Ohio State Reports	Ohio St., Ohio St.2d
	Ohio Appellate Reports	Ohio App., Ohio App.2d
	Ohio Miscellaneous	Ohio Misc.
	Ohio Opinions	Ohio Op., Ohio Op. 2d, Ohio Op. 3d
Oklahoma	Oklahoma Reports	Okla.
Oregon	Oregon Reports	Or.
	Oregon Reports, Court of Appeals	Or.App.
Pennsylvania	Pennsylvania State Reports	Pa.
	Pennsylvania Superior Court Reports	Pa.Super.
Rhode Island	Rhode Island Reports	R.I.
South Carolina	South Carolina Reports	S.C.
South Dakota	South Dakota Reports	S.D.
Tennessee	Tennessee Reports	Tenn.
	Tennessee Appeals	Tenn.App.
Texas	Texas Reports	Tex.
Utah	Utah Reports	Utah
Vermont	Vermont Reports	Vt.
Virginia	Virginia Reports	Va.
Washington	Washington Reports	Wash., Wash.2d
	Washington Appellate Reports	Wash.App.
West Virginia	West Virginia Reports	W.Va.
Wisconsin	Wisconsin Reports	Wis.,Wis.2d
Wyoming	Wyoming Reports	Wy.

The National Reporter System provides the volumes for New York (N.Y.S.) and California (West's California Reporter).

INDICES AND DIGESTS

If you do not have a citation, then you must refer to the statute index. An index is a list of topics, arranged alphabetically, which are fully or partially covered by the particular set of reference books. Listed with topics are the statute numbers relevant to the heading. Research several topic headings (such as Cats, Animals, etc.) until you find what you need. (Even look up the entries under "Dogs" since many of these laws are applicable to cats as well, even though "Cat" may not be expressly mentioned.) Each set of reference books will have its own index.

Some libraries will have an annotated book of statutes. This reference contains summaries of pertinent cases interpreting and applying the relevant statute.

If you do not have a citation when looking for case law, first look in the annotated statute book. If this book is not available, refer to a digest. This is a reference book arranged by headings. Under each heading is a compilation of case summations. If you have trouble finding a proper heading, refer to the index.

USE THE MOST RECENT CITATIONS

Read the most recent cases and statutes you can find. Law cited in an older case or statute may not be valid any more. So when using any reference work, check the pocket part or the supplement. The pocket part is a softcover pamphlet, inserted in the front or back cover of the book. A supplement is a softcover book located either next to the individual volume or at the end of the particular set of reference works. Since pocket parts and supplements are updated annually, they contain the most recent laws.

LEGAL DEFINITIONS

Cases and statutes may include unfamiliar legal language. Or, a seemingly common word or phrase may have a precise and surprising legal definition. It is important to use a word

Utilize a variety of reference materials to be sure you understand the precise legal meaning of a word or phrase.

or phrase in its proper legal context. Therefore, look up definitions in a legal dictionary, not merely a standard dictionary. Unlike a standard dictionary, a legal dictionary defines phrases as well as words.

There is no better place to discover how a term is applied in your jurisdiction than to read the relevant case law. Analyze how a word or phrase is interpreted in several cases to be sure you have a sound understanding.

OTHER REFERENCE SOURCES

Special programs for legal research, Lexis® and Westlaw®, are available on computer. Some libraries have these computer facilities. However, a fee may be involved. If you want some work done on the computer, you must do thorough research first. Information put into the computer must be precise—and the more precise it is, the less time spent on the computer and the lower the cost.

Periodicals are useful resource guides. Newspapers and magazines provide an abundance of information about many topics dealing with cats. They often discuss changes and trends in the law before the information is even available in official form. Always remember that a librarian is always willing to help you find what you need. Do not be afraid to ask.

CHANGING THE LAW

You may be dissatisfied with the laws of your state or municipality. Do not be disgruntled, but do your best to change them. You can advocate for new laws, or broaden, restrict, or eliminate existing laws by writing or lobbying your local representatives. Get the backing of other citizens and animal groups that support your views. With the help of an attorney, a law may be challenged in court.

Your cat is your personal property and, as such, is protected by laws prohibiting a person from injuring, taking, or destroying the personal property of another.

Cats Are Property

A cat is personal property and properly considered a thing of value. *Ford v. Glennon,* 74 Conn. 6, 49 A. 189 (1901). This fact has a lot of legal implications. For instance, since a cat is property and not a person, it has no legal rights of its own. A cat can neither sue nor be sued.

Since property rights exist in a pet cat, Ga. Code Ann. §44-1-8, its owner has legally enforceable rights. All remedies given for the recovery of personal property and of damages sustained are available to a cat owner. N.M. Stat. Ann. §77-1-1.

The law prohibits a person from injuring, taking, or destroying the property of another. So an owner who has a property interest in a cat that is killed, stolen, or injured is entitled to bring a civil action, *Helsel v. Fletcher,* 98 Okla. 285, 225 P. 514 (1914), to regain possession, *Livengood v. Markusson,* 31 Ohio 183, 164 N.E. 61 (1928), or to receive adequate compensation. A person who wrongfully obtains, keeps, or destroys another's cat may be guilty of theft, Minn. Stat. Ann. §609.52, and is subject to a fine or imprisonment. Vt. Stat. Ann. tit. 13, §481. However, a person has a right to use whatever force is reasonably necessary under the circumstances to protect himself, *State v. Spencer,* 20 N.J. Misc. 487, 29 A.2d 398 (1942), the safety of the public, Nev. Rev. Stat. §575.020, and protected species of birds, N.Y. Envtl. Conserv. Law § 11-0529, from an attack by a cat.

A household cat is considered to be a domestic, rather than a wild, animal. Many states have laws that hold a dog owner liable if his dog kills, injures, or worries domestic animals. Hence, a dog owner may be liable if his animal kills or injures a pet cat. *Thurston v. Carter,* 112 Me. 361, 92 A. 295 (1914). Additionally, a cat owner may be allowed to use reasonable measures to protect his cat from the menacing of a dog. However, if the dog is killed, the cat owner must show that he was adequately justified in taking such action or he will be responsible for the value of the dog. *Ford v. Glennon*, 74 Conn. 6, 49 A. 189 (1901).

An owner's property right in his pet is qualified, though. It is subject to the reasonable demands of society. *Central Westchester Humane Soc. v. Hilleboe*, 202 Misc. 881, 116 N.Y.S.2d 403 (1952). For a cat owner to enforce his rights as an owner of property, the cat may need to be licensed. An owner of an unlicensed cat may not be afforded any protection under the law because a law may define only licensed cats as personal property. Rights may even be lost if a licensed cat is not wearing its license. An owner of a kitten, whose young cat does not yet require a license, should still benefit from the property laws concerning cats.

DAMAGES

A cat owner will probably be able to collect damages from someone who intentionally or negligently kills or injures the cat. If the cat owner is partially responsible for the cat's actions, the damage award may be reduced in relation to the proportion of the owner's fault. Liability will not attach if the cat was killed or injured while attacking a person, property, or livestock, or if the cat was lawfully impounded and destroyed.

Damages typically include actual, out-of-pocket expenses, such as medical costs. But other criteria may have some bearing as well. Consider the market value and the age of the cat. Its type, traits, pedigree, and purchase price are all legitimate concerns. Other considerations include registration, breeding value, cost of replacement, the difference between the value of the cat before and after injury, and if the cat was expecting a litter. The personal value of the cat to its owner may or may not have merit. *Zitter*, Measure, Elements, And Amount of Damages Killing or Injuring Cat, 8 A.L.R.4th 1287.

The market value and age of a cat are but two of many considerations that may be evaluated in a damage suit.

A person who intentionally kills or injures a cat may be liable to the cat's owner for damages. He may also be violating anti-cruelty laws.

Some jurisdictions allow the cat owner to recover for mental anguish. The owner may not even have to prove actual ownership, only possession of the animal. *Peloquin v. Calcasieu Parish Police Jury*, 367 So.2d 1246, aff'd, 378 So.2d 560 (La. Ct. App. 1979). Other jurisdictions deny recovery for mental distress, even if the owner witnessed the gruesome death of his pet. *Buchanan v. Stout*, 123 App.Div. 648, 108 N.Y.S. 38, aff'd, 139 App.Div. 204, 123 N.Y.S. 724 (1908). The court reasoned that the cat owner was not in any danger of personal injury herself.

A person who intentionally kills or injures a cat, exhibiting a willful or reckless disregard for the rights of its owner, may be liable for punitive damages. An animal warden who intentionally killed a pet cat in violation of state and city laws was required to pay punitive damages to the owner. *Wilson v. City of Eagan*, 297 N.W.2d 146, 8 A.L.R.4th 1277 (Minn. 1980). Such punitive damages are awarded in addition to an amount considered adequate compensation to the owner. They are intended to punish the wrongdoer for his deliberately malicious conduct.

PRODUCT LIABILITY

A cat may have suffered injury due to a defect in a product. An example may be death from a contaminant in food. A claim such as this is based on product liability. The manufacturer, distributor, wholesaler, or retailer may be held liable on a number of legal theories. First, he may be strictly liable; he is accountable even though there was no fault on his part. Second, he may be held accountable due to negligence; a reasonable person should have foreseen the risk of harm. Third, he may be accountable due to a breach of warranty; the product should have been fit for normal use. Or fourth, he may be liable due to intentional acts; he knew the injuries were substantially certain to result.

A cat can inherit neither money nor property under your will. There are other ways to ensure that your cat will be cared for after your death.

WILLS

Since a cat is not a person, it cannot be a beneficiary of a will. It cannot inherit money or other property. If you want your cat to be cared for after your death, you must designate a new owner for the cat in a will, just as you would with any other property. Discuss the provision with the person you intend to be the new owner. Be sure the person you designate in the will as the new owner really wants the cat and is able to care for it.

It is also wise to leave money to the new owner to care for your cat. Be sure to consider medical expenses because as your cat gets older its veterinary bills will increase. An alternative is to leave money to the veterinarian. The dollar amount and the services to be rendered should be arranged with the doctor. The will can designate that any money remaining when the cat dies goes to the veterinarian, to another person, or wherever you like.

A court will not enforce a will provision that bequeaths money or property to a cat. Since property cannot inherit property, the cat will not inherit anything. The money or property will be distributed according to the state laws governing succession. Of course, this legal distribution is not likely to be what the testator had in mind.

However, a bequest for the care and protection of cats by founding a cattery may be a proper charitable gift. *Shannon v. Eno,* 120 Conn. 77, 179 A. 479 (1935).

DIVORCE

A cat may be contested property in a divorce proceeding. A court will determine custody and visitation rights.

INSURANCE

Your cat may be a pedigreed purebred champion or otherwise unusually valuable. Just like any other property, you can get an insurance policy for your cat. The carrier may reimburse you for the value of the cat. The insurance company

Cats that are the result of genetic engineering may be patentable.

will also be the party responsible to bring suit against the person that harmed the cat.

TAX DEDUCTION

No matter how much a cat is considered a part of the family, the Internal Revenue Service will not permit an owner to list a cat as a dependent, nor can a cat ever be claimed as a medical expense.

TAKING OF PROPERTY

Property cannot be taken from an owner without due process of the law. This means that the cat owner must have notice, and possibly be given a hearing, before his property is taken or destroyed. Therefore, before a cat can be impounded, killed, or offered for adoption, its owner must be given adequate notice. The amount of time considered adequate notice varies from place to place and may depend on whether or not the cat is licensed.

PATENTS

There is a new trend emerging in the law regarding animal patents. A patent is legal property. In 1988, Harvard University in Cambridge, Massachusetts, obtained the first patent ever granted for an animal. Since then, the number of pending applications for animal life forms has surged. This patenting of genetic engineering may mean that new cat breeds will be patented. Royalties may have to be paid each time a patented animal gives birth or generates income.

VICIOUS CATS

Once a cat has bitten a person or exhibited menacing behavior, it may officially be declared vicious. Usually a hearing is held to determine if a cat is vicious.

Owners of vicious cats may be required to take strict measures to control their cats. A vicious cat may have to be securely confined indoors or enclosed outside in a locked pen. When the cat is in any public place or common area (such as

An owner should not conceal the fact that his cat has vicious tendencies. Precautions must be taken to prevent injury.

the hallway of an apartment building), it must be leashed and muzzled. If the cat is in a motor vehicle, the vehicle must be locked and have a closed roof.

The cat may have to be spayed or neutered at the owner's expense. Owning or harboring a vicious cat may be considered a nuisance.

The law may bar a person younger than 18 years old from owning a vicious cat. The owner may be required to have liability insurance for the cat. Signs may be necessary to warn the public that a vicious cat is on the premises. Such a sign may have to contain a symbol designed to inform children that a dangerous cat is present.

An owner who fails to comply with the law may be fined or imprisoned. He may also be liable for double or triple the amount of damage caused by the cat. A vicious cat that is considered a serious danger may be impounded and killed. Its owner is entitled to notice and a hearing.

You should be aware that licensed and unlicensed cats may be given different treatment under the law.

General Guidelines for Cat Owners

Licenses

Some jurisdictions require pet cats to have a license. Wis. Stat. Ann. §59.877. A license involves a fee. It usually has to be renewed periodically. It should be worn by the cat at all times. In most areas, a cat license can be gotten by mail.

A license may be valid throughout the entire state. Some licenses, though, are good only in the city or county that issued them. If you move to another state, your cat will almost surely need a new license. If the cat gets a new owner, the old license may be transferable, or a new license may be required.

Kittens under a certain age are exempt from the licensing requirements. A license may cost less for a spayed or neutered cat, or a cat belonging to an old or disabled person. A special breeder, hobby, or cattery license may be in order if you breed, sell, or keep more than a certain number of cats. A licensed cattery may not be required to obtain a license tag for each individual cat. Cal. Food & Agric. Code §31751.6.

To find out where to get a license, talk to your pet shop owner, veterinarian, city or county officials, the animal control or health department, or look in the telephone book.

Licensed and unlicensed cats may be accorded different treatment under the law. You may not be able to take advantage of the property rights that attach to cats. Any unlicensed cat, or an unlicensed cat running at large, may be impounded, then destroyed or offered for adoption. Unlicensed cats that are impounded are killed or sold sooner than licensed cats, because local authorities are unable to trace ownership. Furthermore, some localities may permit the

Required vaccinations vary from area to area. It may be necessary for a cat to wear a vaccination tag at all times.

killing of an unlicensed cat, or a licensed cat not wearing its license, at any time. Yet a cat wearing a license may be killed only if it is attacking a person, property, or livestock.

If your cat is lost or stolen, it will be harder to find if it does not have a license. An owner of an unlicensed cat may be subject to a fine or penalty.

VACCINATIONS

A current rabies vaccination is a common requirement in most locales. Ark. Stat. Ann. §20-19-202. The law may demand that a cat have a rabies vaccination in order to get a license. Wis. Stat. Ann. §59.877. A free anti-rabies clinic may be offered periodically. D.C. Code Ann. §6-1003. Other injections, such as a distemper shot, may be required as well.

A veterinarian administering shots may be required to issue a report to the local authorities. This is one way the government makes sure that owners register their cats. Kittens under a certain age are not required to be vaccinated. Proof of current vaccinations may be necessary before you can transport your cat to another state or country. The owner of a cat not wearing a vaccination tag may be fined, Ala. Code §3-7-6, and the cat may be impounded, Ala. Code §3-7-8.

An unvaccinated cat that bites a person will probably have to be quarantined in a pound or veterinary hospital. A vaccinated cat may be permitted to be quarantined at the home of its owner. Ariz. Rev. Stat. Ann. §24-372.

SPAYING AND NEUTERING

Some states have established clinics where cats can be spayed or neutered. Conn. Gen. Stat. Ann. §22-380a. Some communities provide free sterilization services on a periodic basis. Others offer low-cost services to owners who meet the eligibility requirements. N.J. Stat. Ann. §4:19A-1. A license tag may cost less for a spayed or neutered cat than for one which has not been fixed. Cal. Food & Agric. Code §31751.5.

CATS AND THE LAW

Some locales require that a cat be on a leash when in public. A vicious cat may have to be muzzled as well.

RUNNING AT LARGE

The law may require a cat to be under the control and surveillance of its owner at all times. The cat owner is responsible to ensure that the cat cannot harm the person or property of another. *Helsel v. Fletcher*, 98 Okla. 285, 225 P. 514, 33 A.L.R. 792 (1914). Such supervision may involve confinement or that the cat be on a leash. An unleashed animal found off the premises of its owner may be considered to be at large. D.C. Code Ann. §6-1001.

The term "run at large" typically means a generalized wandering. It may or may not be applicable to an isolated instance where a cat has been found loose in the neighborhood. *People v. Christo*, 19 N.Y.2d 678, 278 N.Y.S.2d 868, 225 N.E.2d 558 (1967). A cat running at large in violation of the law may be impounded. Ala. Code §3-7-7. A stray cat may be considered a predatory animal and therefore subject to laws governing wildlife. Wyo. Stat §23-1-101.

VEHICLES

A cat should never be left alone in a car. It takes only a few minutes for the heat to become unbearable in the summer, and to drop to freezing in the winter. Some towns actually prohibit a cat from being left alone in a car. An owner may be violating anti-cruelty laws.

A cat traveling in a car or truck should be well behaved. An undisciplined cat can be deadly in a moving vehicle. The cat should be contained in a carrier. Some manufacturers sell seat belts and car seats designed for pets.

HOW MANY CATS ALLOWED?

Many animal lovers have more than one cat. However, some communities restrict the number of cats allowed per household, and some residences refuse to permit cats at all.

These laws are taken quite seriously. If your condominium or apartment lease has a no-pets clause, you can be evicted for harboring a cat. If your residence limits the num-

Your town may have a restriction on the number of cats that can be kept in one household.

ber of cats you can keep, exceeding that number can subject you to a daily fine.

Some communities restrict the number of cats per household. If you want to keep more pets, you may need to apply for a city permit or a cattery or hobbyist license. This may cntail extra fees, rules, and inspections.

An owner may be required to dispose of the number of cats exceeding the allowable limit. Fines and jail sentences can be imposed as well. These enforcement measures can be imposed even if you are caring for someone else's cat only temporarily. Kittens less than a certain age may or may not be excepted.

LOST AND FOUND

If your cat is lost, call any agency you think handles cats. Include the police, health and animal control departments, and humane societies. Listen to local radio stations and read the local newspapers that list found animals. Visit the police station, animal shelter, and city hall where lists may be posted. Some agencies refuse to give out information over the phone. Leave a picture and an accurate description of the cat every place you visit. If at first you are not successful, keep asking around. The cat may show up later.

If you find a cat, attempt to find its owner, or give the cat to the local authorities. If you do not make an effort to return the cat to its owner, you may be liable to the owner for the value of the cat. Some states require you to call the animal control authorities. If the law requires you to turn the cat in to a shelter, ask to have the first chance at adoption.

A pound with custody of the cat is responsible to look for the owner. It probably has a procedure for making a public announcement if the cat is not tagged. Conn. Gen. Stat. Ann. §22-369.

If the cat remains in your possession, check for identification. The cat may have the name and address of its owner on a tag. Call the owner. If the cat has a license tag, call the agency that issued the tag to get the name of the owner.

In the event that your cat becomes lost, you may have to provide a description of his physical appearance to any of several agencies. Remember to note any markings or other characteristics that make his appearance distinctive.

Sick and injured cats are often pound inhabitants.

Ask local residents if they recognize the cat. Post signs around the area where the cat was found. Put a notice in the paper and notify the local radio station.

Impoundment laws often give animal control officials the authority to pick up, impound, sell, and destroy cats. However, since a pet cat is considered the personal property of its owner, it cannot be confiscated without notice, and possibly a hearing. A pound is obligated to provide proper care and maintenance to its inhabitants during the length of their stay. Ariz. Rev. Stat. Ann. §24-371.

An owner's property rights may be lost, though, under certain conditions. Any unlicensed cat, or a cat running at large without a vaccination tag, or running at large without a license tag may be impounded without first notifying its owner. Once impounded, the pound must attempt to notify the owner. Ala. Code §3-7-8.

Cats running around loose are typical pound inhabitants. Injured, abandoned, and vicious cats also end up at the pound. A cat that has bitten a person, caused damage, or been declared a nuisance can be taken from its owner and impounded. An owner who has his cat in his possession, though, is entitled to be notified before the cat is seized. An owner must be notified again before the cat is destroyed. Most jurisdictions even give the owner a chance in court to argue that the cat should not be killed.

A pound is required to keep the cat for a prescribed period of time before it can take action. The holding time can vary anywhere from one to 14 days. The holding period may not be applicable to severely injured, seriously ill, or newborn kittens. Cal. Food & Agric. Code §31752.

To reclaim the cat, an owner may have to have the cat licensed, vaccinated, spayed or neutered, to pay a fine and a charge for every day that the cat was kept. Ala. Code §3-7-8. If the owner does not claim the cat, it can be sold, offered for adoption, or killed in a humane manner.

Some localities declare it unlawful to knowingly sell or give an impounded cat for experimentation. Others permit a

Insurance is available to cover a cat's medical expenses, as well as the cost of damage done by a cat.

cat to be sold to a research or teaching facility. That facility may have to be certified by the state. Ohio Rev. Code Ann. §955.16(B). A pound that turns cats over for research may have to post a sign stating as much. Cal. Civ. Code §1834.7.

A pound can make a new owner have the cat spayed or neutered. Ark. Stat. Ann. §20-19-103. The adoption fee may include the price of required vaccinations.

ANIMAL CONTROL AUTHORITIES

Cat laws may be enforced by any number of agencies. These include the police, a humane society, an animal control center, or a health department. The officers are empowered to summon and arrest violators. N.Y. Agric. & Mkts. Law §371.

No matter which organization is responsible for enforcing the law, all of them must respect the legal rights of an owner. If your cat is wrongfully impounded and is sold, destroyed, suffers some injury, or becomes ill as a result, you may be able to sue. You must be able to prove that you did not receive the proper notice, that the animal was improperly taken, or that it was kept after you tried to get it out. If the authorities acted in good faith and with due care pursuant to the law, chances are that they will not be civilly or criminally liable for their actions. Fla. Stat. Ann. §828.05.

INSURANCE

Your cat may be particularly valuable. You can get insurance that will compensate you for the cost of injury or death to the cat.

Liability insurance can be purchased; some policies will pay for any damage or injury done by your cat, as well as any injury sustained by your pet. It is wise to have liability coverage for every cat. Given the right circumstances, any cat can cause harm.

You may want to get a health insurance policy for your cat. This insurance will pay for medical expenses, including doctor bills, hospital fees, and medications. Medical atten-

Because pets display unconditional love and affection, caring for a cat may have therapeutic benefits; both physical and mental health may be enhanced.

tion required for sickly or older cats can be quite expensive. Some states limit the types of insurance firms that can offer pet health insurance. N.J. Stat. Ann. §17:46-D.

BURIAL

Contact your local animal control authority for information on how to dispose of your cat's remains. Although many cat owners bury their pet in their own yard, many towns have ordinances against this. The carcass cannot be left in a waterway, on public property, or on a public road, Fla. Stat. Ann. §823.041, unless the area is a public dump or other such facility. The cat may have to be brought to a cemetery. Some jurisdictions permit burning the carcass, Fla. Stat. Ann. §823.041; others forbid it, Idaho Code §18-5803. The wisest thing to do is to have your vet handle the burial. Some towns will dispose of the cat for a fee.

Coping with the loss of a loved pet can be stressful. The feelings of grief and loss can last for a long time. Sometimes friends and family display little sympathy to the pet owner. Bide-A-Wee provides free counseling for bereaved pet owners. Information on how to cope with pet loss and bereavement is available from:

Delta Society
P.O. Box 1080
Renton, WA 98057
(206) 226-7357
Fax: (206) 235-1076

THERAPY

When people talk to people, their blood pressure rises. Yet when people talk to animals, their blood pressure goes down. Animals and humans relate so well because animals give unconditional love and affection. This non-judgmental interaction has a therapeutic effect on disturbed, disabled, convalescing, or confined individuals. Caring for an animal raises morale and social activity, and actually gives some people a reason to live.

Cats, like many other kinds of animals, are being used successfully in pet therapy programs for the sick and the elderly.

Therefore, an assortment of animals, including cats, dogs, fish, guinea pigs and other domestic pets, are used in a variety of therapy programs. Many health care facilities, including hospitals, day care centers, psychiatric wards, abuse shelters and nursing homes, with programs for the sick, the elderly, and the mentally disabled, utilize therapy or social dogs in their programs. A health-related facility may be permitted to board cats if the general well being of the residents would be promoted. N.Y. Pub. Health Law §2803-h. Even prison inmates are allowed to have cats visit. Some institutions allow patients to have visits from their own household pets.

Laws are not required for a facility in your state to allow pets. There are probably no laws against such an activity. The decision is up to the administrators of the particular institution. An arrangement must be made between the institution and a facility that will provide the animals.

The Delta Society offers for sale a wide variety of resource materials, such as books, journals, slides, video tapes, and audio tapes. The materials discuss pets and the elderly, animal assistance programs, prison programs, therapy programs, as well as many other animal-related topics. For further information, contact:

Delta Society
P.O. Box 1080
Renton, WA 98057
(206) 226-7357
Fax: (206) 235-1076

The wise cat owner will take sensible measures to prevent his pet from injuring another person.

Owner Liability

Personal Injury; Property Damage; Nuisance

An owner is legally responsible for controlling his animal. An owner may be liable for any personal injury or property damage caused by his pet. Given the right circumstances, any cat can injure or destroy. Therefore, a prudent owner will take precautionary measures to prevent his cat from causing harm. A cat owner who violates the law may be guilty of a felony or a misdemeanor, fined or imprisoned.

DAMAGES

If injury or damage occurs, an owner may have to pay medical expenses. This can include costs for doctors, hospitals, medications, physical therapy, and counseling. A victim may also be entitled to loss of earnings if he was out of work due to his injury. The time off may involve both treatment and recuperation.

Some courts may award compensation for pain and suffering experienced by the victim. The amount of the award can vary tremendously depending on the circumstance because it is difficult to calculate the cost specifically. Sometimes a spouse or close relative can receive compensation as well. The theory is loss of service of the injured person. Loss of service is not limited to economics; it may also include loss of companionship.

If the fault on the part of the owner is particularly shocking or reckless, a court may double or even triple the damage award. Additionally, the victim may be entitled to punitive damages. This recovery punishes the owner's poor conduct by making him pay even more than the amount considered adequate compensation to the victim. The financial status of the owner can be taken into account when establishing a punitive damage award.

The potential reimbursement costs for damage or injury caused by a cat can be extensive. A wise pet owner will take measures to minimize his risk.

LEGAL THEORIES

There are several legal theories under which a cat owner may be found liable for his pet's acts. One or more theories may be applicable in your state.

Common Law

The common law is that body of law which is derived from case decisions. According to the common law, owners of animals *ferae naturae* (wild animals), such as tigers, elephants, gorillas, and bears, assume absolute liability for these animals. An owner keeps them at his peril; negligence on the part of the owner is presumed.

Animals *manuetae naturae* are animals which have been domesticated by man for centuries. They are regarded as inherently safe; there is no presumption that they are dangerous to man. *Talley v. Travelers Ins. Co.*, 197 So.2d 92 (La. Ct. App. 1967). However, if a domestic animal manifests a vicious temperament, an owner retains it at his peril. *Marsh v. Snyder*, 52 So.2d 605 (La. Ct. App. 1951).

The common household varieties of cats are regarded as domestic, Pa. Stat. Ann. tit. 3, §331, rather than wild animals. They are not regarded as naturally dangerous to man. As such, an owner may have to have notice of his cat's dangerous propensities in order to be deemed liable for injuries caused by the cat. *Bernke v. Stepp*, 109 Okla. 119, 184 P.2d 615 (1947). If a cat who did not previously display vicious tendencies subsequently acts dangerously, the owner may not be liable for damages. *Marsalis v. La Salle*, 94 So.2d 120 La. Ct. App. 1957).

Even a gentle cat may exhibit savage behavior when protecting its kittens. However, a cat with young is still considered a domestic pet. Its owner is not strictly liable for damage caused by his pet merely because it has kittens. *Clinton v. J. Lyons & Co.*, [1912] 3 K.B. 198. However, liability may be imposed in a situation whereby a store owner knows that some of his customers enter with their cats. The shopkeeper may be negligent in exposing his customers to the vicious-

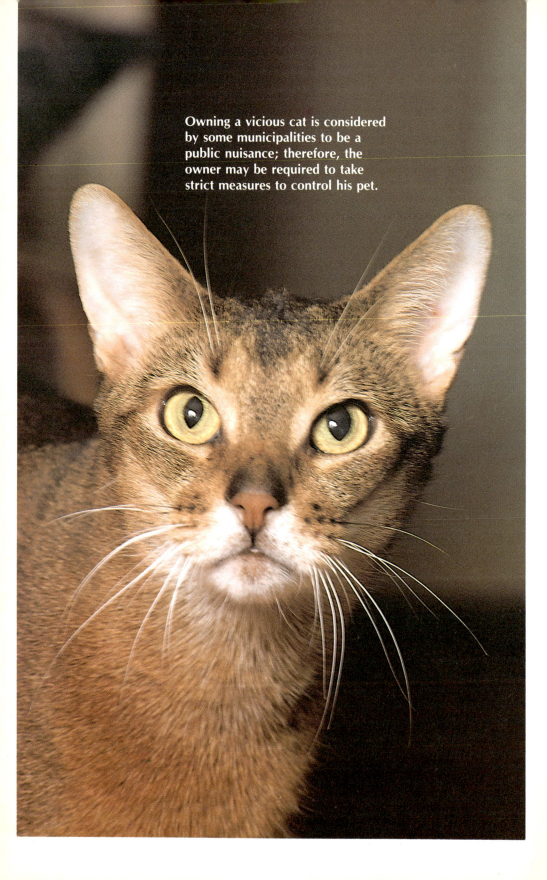

Owning a vicious cat is considered by some municipalities to be a public nuisance; therefore, the owner may be required to take strict measures to control his pet.

ness of his cat which had a kitten. *Gardner v. H. C. Bohack Co.*, 166 N.Y.S. 476 (1917).

The common law allows a cat not necessarily a free bite, but one chance to exhibit dangerous behavior before its owner is legally responsible for injury caused by the cat. Thereafter, the owner is on notice that the cat is prone to bite or otherwise cause injury. Sometimes the common law language uses the term "vicious." This just means that the cat is likely to cause harm; it does not refer to the cat's overall temperament.

Cat laws, state statutes and local ordinances, may have modified the common law in your jurisdiction. The local law may impose absolute liability, regardless of fault, on the owner for any injury or damage caused by the pet. Or, some other legal theories may be appropriate. Check the appropriate reference sources.

Read the statute carefully. The injured party must show that all the elements required by the law have been met. In some states, the burden of proof is on the owner to prove that he was not at fault. Other statutes shift the burden of proof to the victim; he must prove that he was not at fault.

When evaluating a statute, do not limit yourself to a literal reading, though. It is important to research the case decisions because the court may have a different interpretation of the law than you do. For example, a statute often uses a term, such as owner, but does not define it. You may assume that the owner is the person with legal title. However, the definition of an owner, as determined in the case law, may be broad enough to include the legal owner, as well as anyone who cares for, harbors, or has custody of the cat.

Another example is that case law may restrict an owner's defenses even though the statute does not. So, for a thorough analysis, your legal research must encompass the case law as well as the statutory law.

Vicious Cats

Once a cat has bitten a person or exhibited menacing behavior, it may be declared vicious. Bear in mind that the cat

Proper legal research involves a lot of time and effort.

does not have to have caused actual injury to be considered vicious. Its owner merely needs to have sufficient notice that the cat has dangerous tendencies. Thereafter, the owner may be liable for any damages caused by the vicious cat. *Marsalis v. La Salle*, 94 So.2d 120 (La. Ct. App. 1957). Negligence on the part of the owner may be presumed. The animal control authorities may be required to dispose of a cat determined to be vicious. S.D. Codified Laws Ann. §7-12-29.

In proving a vicious propensity, it may be sufficient for the victim of an attack to show that, under the law, the cat was required to be on a leash, and at the time of the event, the cat was not on a leash. Ga. Code Ann. §51-2-7. In some jurisdictions, the burden of proving lack of knowledge that the cat was vicious may be on the owner.

Owners of vicious cats may be required to take strict measures to control their cats. A vicious cat may have to be securely confined to its owner's property. N.C. Gen. Stat. §130A-200. When the cat is in any public place or common area it may have to be leashed, Ill. Ann. Stat. ch. 8, §365, and muzzled. If the cat is in a motor vehicle, the vehicle must be locked and have a closed roof.

The cat may have to be spayed or neutered at the owner's expense. Owning or harboring a vicious cat may be considered a nuisance. Signs may be necessary to warn the public that a vicious cat is on the premises. Such a sign may have to contain a symbol designed to inform children that a dangerous cat is present.

An owner who fails to comply with the law may be fined or imprisoned. He may also be liable for double or triple the amount of damage caused by the cat. A vicious cat that is considered a serious danger may be impounded and killed. Its owner, though, is entitled to notice and a hearing.

Negligence

If the injured party can show that the pet owner was unreasonably careless in controlling the cat, compensation may

Not all cats and dogs get along as nicely as this. Exercise caution when introducing your feline to another animal to decrease the chance of a confrontation.

be awarded for harm that was reasonably foreseeable as a result. The court may even presume negligence on the part of the owner if the cat is known to have dangerous propensities. If a court determines that a cat owner exercised due care in restraining the cat, though, even if that cat was known to be vicious, the court may refuse to impose liability. *Bischoff v. Cheney*, 89 Conn. 1, 92 A. 660 (1914).

Nuisance

A cat may not have caused physical damage or injury, but it may be a nuisance. A nuisance can be characterized as anything which repeatedly causes a substantial and unreasonable or unlawful annoyance, disturbance, inconvenience or damage to another. For instance, a cat that caterwauls incessantly or late at night may be a nuisance. For an owner who lives in an apartment, a cat deemed a nuisance can be sufficient grounds for an owner to be sued or evicted.

The mere possession of cats does not necessarily create a nuisance. *People v. Cooper*, 64 Cal.App.2d, 149 P.2d 86 (1944). Determining a nuisance may depend on the number and the manner in which the cats are kept. Having 40 cats on the premises, *Boudinot v. State*, 340 P.2d 268, 73 A.L.R.2d 1027 (Okla. 1959), and allowing diseased cats to stray and destroy birds, *People v. Ehrlich*, 14 N.Y.S.2d 125 (1939), were considered public nuisances by the courts.

DEFENSES

The owner has some defenses that he can plead. The defenses acceptable in a court vary from state to state. In addition, the right to declare a particular defense may be governed by the legal theory asserted by the injured party. For instance, contributory negligence may be an acceptable defense against an attack under the common law, but it may be barred as a defense against a state statute.

No matter how attractive your cat is, it may still be considered a nuisance.

A cat owner may exculpate himself by proving that the harm arose from an independent cause, such as fault on the part of the victim or of a third party for which the owner is not responsible. However, such fault must be a substantial factor in bringing about the injury. *Martinez v. Modenbach*, 396 So.2d 471 (La. Ct. App. 1981).

Negligence

The owner may offer proof of contributory or comparative negligence on the part of the victim. This means that the injured party displayed conduct falling below that of a reasonable person. He was injured, at least partly, due to his own careless behavior. A woman was not allowed to recover for injuries she sustained from a cat. The woman reached down to touch the cat after the woman's dog and the cat had a fight. The cat scratched her. The court reasoned that any reasonable person would have kept herself and her dog away from the cat. Instead, the woman unnecessarily exposed herself to danger and so was contributorily negligent. *Goodwin v. E. B. Nelson Grocery Co.*, 239 Mass. 232, 132 N.E. 51 (1921).

Contributory negligence is a complete bar to recovery. The doctrine of comparative negligence simply reduces the amount of the award the victim can collect.

Attractive Nuisance

The definition of an attractive nuisance is as follows: 1) there exists an artificial condition on the land, 2) which is dangerous, 3) of which the landowner is or should be aware, 4) the owner knows or should know that children visit the property, 5) the children do not appreciate the risk of harm, and 6) the expense of remedying the situation is slight compared to the magnitude of risk. Some courts have considered the applicability of this doctrine to animal injuries, but most of them have rejected the concept. *Trenkner*, Animals As Attractive Nuisance, 64 A.L.R.3d 1069.

A cat owner may not be responsible for his cat's injuring a person who purposefully provoked the animal to the point of rage.

The reasoning is that not everything attractive to a child is an attractive nuisance. Domestic animals are simply too common to be inherently dangerous, even to a child. *Dykes v. Alexander*, 411 S.W.2d 47 (Ky. 1967). However, a domestic animal that is known to be dangerous and is likely to cause injury may be classified as an attractive nuisance. *Rolen v. Maryland Casualty Co.*, 240 So.2d 42 (La. Ct. App. 1970).

Assumption of Risk

The owner may escape liability by asserting assumption of risk by the victim. In this situation, the victim may not recover for damages if he voluntarily, knowingly, and purposefully exposes himself to a known and appreciated danger. *Daniel v. Cambridge Mut. Fire Ins. Co.*, 368 So.2d 810 (La. Ct App. 1979). The cat owner must prove that the injured party had knowledge of the facts, knew of the dangerous condition, appreciated the nature and extent of the risk, and voluntarily exposed himself to it thereby assuming the risk. This is one situation when posting a "Beware of Cat" sign may come into play.

Veterinarians and staff members bitten when treating a cat may have assumed the risk. They knew of the danger and acted deliberately in treating the cat.

Provocation

Another defense is intentional provocation of the cat by the victim. Here, the injured party acted purposefully in irritating, inciting, or arousing rage in the cat. Provocation may not have to be deliberate. For example, someone may accidentally step on a cat's tail. A court may consider that a veterinarian, in his treatment of the cat, provoked it to bite. An owner, though, cannot conceal the fact that his cat is vicious.

Unlawful Acts

In some states, a victim engaged in an unlawful act at the time of the injury may not recover anything from the cat

A cat owner may not be responsible for injuries incurred by a trespasser who entered the premises at his own risk.

owner. A statute may require the victim to prove he was not breaking the law; the owner does not have to prove the victim was doing an illegal act. If the victim cannot prove his good conduct, there is no recovery.

Trespassing

Some states do not protect trespassers who are injured by a cat. A trespasser is someone on your property who has not been invited. However, an invitation does not have to be explicit; it can be implied. Anyone that you can reasonably expect to be on your property, such as a delivery person or mail carrier, has an implied invitation, unless warnings are posted to the contrary.

Some courts permit an owner to raise the defenses of contributory or comparative negligence, or assumption of the risk against the claims of a trespasser. The trespasser may be allowed to show that the owner acted unreasonably under the circumstances.

Some states permit a trespasser to sue only if the landowner knew that the intruder was on the property. The landowner is responsible only if he knew of the intruder's presence, and intentionally caused harm or failed to warn of danger.

In particular, children often are deemed to have an implied invitation to enter property. Children do not possess the reasoning capabilities of adults. Therefore, an adult bears a heavy burden of protecting children from a cat.

Statute of Limitations

Different legal theories have different statutes of limitations (time limits). These statutes establish a particular time in which suit must be brought. For example, one law may require a suit to be filed within one year from the date of the injury while another law may have a two year limit. Check the laws of your jurisdiction. If you intend to sue, file the action as soon as possible to avoid dismissal on the grounds that the statute of limitations has run out.

A cat owner may or may not be responsible for damages if his cat worries, injures, or kills livestock.

PREVENTING INJURY

If you are a cat owner, the best way to avoid liability is to prevent injury. Adhere to a few common sense rules to keep risk of harm to a minimum.

No matter how small, old or timid your cat is, it can hurt someone, damage property, or be a nuisance. Any cat may bite or scratch if it is threatened, or if it is protecting its owner, its kittens, or its food. Or a cat running into the street may startle an unsuspecting driver and result in injury. Therefore, the best idea is to keep your cat securely contained in the house or yard. Be sure it cannot escape to scare or otherwise get in the way of strangers. Post warning signs that alert passers-by that a cat is present. The owner must be in control at all times.

Lastly, keep the cat's license and vaccinations up-to-date. If your cat does manage to get free, its return will be more expedient if it is properly identified. The less time out of your care, the less time the cat has to cause trouble. And should the cat bite someone, the cat will not need to be quarantined if its rabies vaccine is current.

RESPONSIBILITY RESTS WITH OWNERS

Typically it is the cat's legal owner who is responsible for the actions of his pet. However, someone else, or more than one person, may be liable. For instance, a cat may have more than one owner, or someone other than the owner may have custody of the cat.

A keeper is a person who cares for, manages, or possesses the cat. Often the owner and the keeper are the same person, but sometimes they are not. The law may establish that the owner, the keeper, and anyone else who permits the animal to remain on his premises are liable. Ala. Code §3-7-1; Ill. Stat. Ann. Ch. 8, §353. Some jurisdictions strictly limit responsibility to the owner.

A cat owner may be under 18 years of age. In such a situation, the minor's parents or legal guardian may be responsible for any injury or damage caused by the cat. A court may impose liability under one of several legal theories. The parents may be considered the keepers of the cat; they may be deemed responsible for damage caused by their minor child; or the law may expressly state that the parents of a minor are responsible for the cat.

Under certain circumstances, liability may be imposed on a landlord. The landlord must have known that a tenant's cat was dangerous, was capable of removing the cat, and did nothing about it. A landlord who knows that a tenant has a vicious cat must take reasonable measures to protect people who might be on the premises from being attacked by the cat. Precautionary provisions may be included in the lease.

INSURANCE

The cost of the potential damage and injury inflicted by a cat can be substantial. A wise owner will check to see that his homeowner's or renter's policy covers his cat. A cat that has a menacing behavior should have its own insurance coverage.

A typical homeowner's or renter's insurance plan covers any damage caused by the policy holder's negligence. This coverage often extends to incidents that take place away from the owner's property, even if a vehicle is involved. If the policy does not extend to vehicular events, look to your auto insurance plan. Some insurance companies refuse to issue a policy altogether if a vicious cat lives in the home.

Often a plan limits its coverage to the first instance of harm caused by a cat. After that, the owner must pay out of his own pocket. Other companies exclude certain types of cat-related harm from their coverage. This is why it is important to read your policy carefully. If you do not understand the terms, call your agent for an explanation. It is important to know your liability before an accident occurs.

If your home and auto insurance do not extend to cat-related injuries, or you think the coverage is not broad enough, buy insurance for your pet. Take out insurance that will protect you and the cat while at home and away. Get a policy that will pay for your cat's medical expenses as well.

Buying, Selling, and Breeding

If you regularly sell, keep, or breed more than a certain number of cats, you may need a cattery, hobbyist, or breeder's license.

Even if the cat that you want to purchase appears to be in good health, you should request that the purchase be subject to a satisfactory health check by a veterinarian.

Most of the laws regulating buyers, sellers, and breeders of cats pertain to dealers. A dealer is a person who buys and sells cats in the regular course of his business. The definition of a dealer may include breeders, pet shops, and brokers. An owner who sells the family pet's kittens at a yard sale is not covered. However, some laws do encompass the occasional seller. The law may deal more strictly with someone engaged in business, but an individual still has responsibility as well.

If you regularly sell, keep, or breed more than a certain number of cats, you may need a cattery, hobbyist, or breeder's license. Kittens may or may not be included in this number. Usually diseased cats, and cats under a specified age (usually eight weeks) cannot be sold.

If you are the buyer, insist that the sale of a cat is subject to a satisfactory health check by a veterinarian. Whether you are the buyer or the seller, put the sales agreement in writing. Until you write it out, you may not realize that you and the other party have different understandings. Both parties should sign the certificate. The agreement should include, but is certainly not limited to, the following disclosures:

1. The breed, sex, age, color, quality, and birth date of the cat
2. The names and addresses of the buyer and the seller
3. The name and address of the breeder
4. The name and address of the party from whom the cat was purchased
5. The pedigree
6. Litter number
7. The name and registration number of the cat
8. The date the dealer took possession
9. The date shipped to the dealer
10. The date of veterinary exams, the name and address of the veterinarian, and any findings and treatments
11. The date and types of vaccinations

12. The behavior (viciousness) and propensities (training) of the cat
13. Any health problems the cat may have
14. Any warranties (guarantees) the seller is making
15. Price

A dissatisfied buyer has a limited period of time, typically 14 days, in which he can return the cat. Within that time, the buyer should be able to return the cat for a refund, or to exchange it for another cat of equivalent value. In some instances, the buyer may be able to keep the cat and recover the difference between the actual value paid and the actual value of the cat received. Cal. Civ. Code §3343. The buyer may also be able to bill the seller for veterinary costs. Some states allow a purchaser several days to return a cat after a veterinarian has certified that the animal is unfit. N.Y. Gen. Bus. Law §742.

PET SHOPS

Anyone who wants to operate as a dealer must obtain a license. 9 C.F.R. §2.1. Compliance with standards for facilities, 9 C.F.R. §2.3, and record keeping requirements, 9 C.F.R. §2.75, as set forth in the Animal Welfare Act must be maintained.

Typically, pet stores must have a veterinarian examine kittens prior to their being offered for sale and at reasonable intervals until sold. The pet shop must ensure that appropriate health care is provided. Usually sick animals and those who have not been examined by a veterinarian must be quarantined. A pet shop cannot sell a cat or kitten unless a health certificate signed by a veterinarian is provided. Mich. Comp. Laws Ann. §287.335a. A cat must be kept a minimum number of days, usually five, before it can be offered for sale. Tenn. Code Ann. §44-17-114.

Some states impose cage labeling requirements. The tag may have to include the supplier's name and address, the sex and breed of the cat, its place and date of birth, the name of its veterinarian, and dates of examination.

Typically, a purchaser has 14 days in which to return a cat suffering from an illness or other condition, existing at the time of the sale, which adversely affects its health. The cat can be exchanged for one of similar value, or the consumer can get a refund for the price of the cat. The law may allow the pet owner to retain the cat. Reimbursement of veterinary fees [up to a certain amount] to certify the cat unfit or to cure it may be recovered. A purchaser may have no legal recourse if he mistreats or neglects the cat.

Some states require pet stores to provide customers with a statement of consumer rights and remedies, N.Y. Gen. Bus. Law §743, and to post a notice. The dealer may be legally obligated to explain the notice orally. The consumer may have to sign a form certifying that he understands his options. Either the dealer or the consumer can initiate legal action.

The purchaser may have to notify the seller of problems within a limited amount of time after receiving veterinary certification. It may be necessary to provide the seller with the telephone number of the doctor.

A pet shop should regularly clean and disinfect all cages, bowls, food bins, utensils, floors, and counter tops. Fecal material should be removed daily. Wire floors or grates lessen the chance of spreading disease. Food should be stored in covered containers. Food must be replaced daily. The water should be clean and fresh. A pet shop that does not provide adequate care may be committing a misdemeanor. Va. Code Ann. §3.1-796.71.

A pet shop is a convenient place from which to purchase a cat. It also has other advantages. A pet shop has good experience with kittens, carries a range of products for cats, and is not looking to sell you a cat at any cost. A pet shop wants your repeated business and so will want to ensure that you remain a satisfied customer.

Before you purchase that special feline, you should be fully aware of all the responsibilities that go along with cat ownership.

All the special qualities of a cat should be included in the sales agreement.

BREEDING

You need to know the law concerning how many cats can be kept. Some municipalities strictly limit the number of cats that can be kept per household. An apartment or condominium may not allow more than one cat, if any at all. If you breach these limits, you may have to get rid of the extra cats or have them impounded. You may also have to pay a fine.

Some cities require you to obtain a hobbyist, breeder, or cattery license. These licenses are probably more expensive than a regular cat license. Your premises may need to meet certain requirements and will be subject to inspection by the authorities.

The law may make an exception for kittens or cats kept only temporarily. However, there may be no exceptions. Familiarize yourself with the law before breeding a cat. This will save you a lot of frustration in the future.

Veterinarians

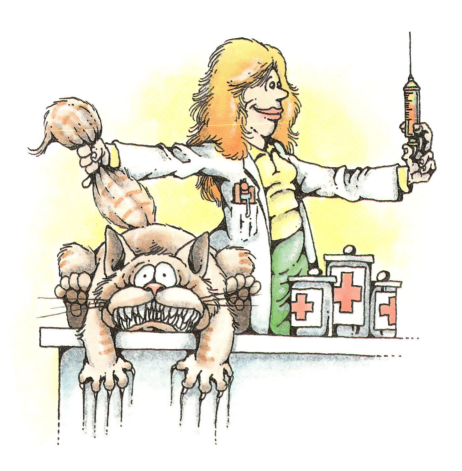

Sometimes, medical treatment for your cat can be costly. Therefore, you might want to explore the benefits of health insurance for your feline.

Your cat is probably like a member of your family, so find a veterinarian whom you trust. You should feel comfortable with the doctor because you will be relying on his professional judgment when it comes to caring for your cat.

A veterinarian should take the time to explain diagnoses, treatments, and costs. If you do not understand, ask questions. Get the specifics in writing if the treatment and costs are extensive. This will avoid unpleasantness in the future. A licensed veterinarian who renders professional services to a cat may be authorized to detain the animal until its owner pays a reasonable fee for the treatment. N.Y. Lien Law §183.

Your cat's medical expenses cannot be deducted from your income tax. However, you can purchase health insurance for your pet. You might want to arrange a lifetime care contract with the veterinarian. The idea is to have the doctor provide medical services to your cat, in exchange for a lump sum, from the time of your death until the cat's death.

A veterinarian can euthanize a sick or older cat at your request. He can also dispose of the cat's remains. A healthy cat probably will not be put to sleep on demand. The veterinarian is likely to suggest alternatives or will try to find a new owner.

A veterinarian is not responsible for a cat indefinitely. A cat that is not retrieved by its owner from the veterinarian's office after a specified amount of time, usually 14 days, is considered abandoned. The doctor should attempt to find a new owner. If a new owner cannot be found, the cat can be destroyed. Cal. Civ. Code §1834.5. The cat must be killed in a humane manner.

If a veterinarian cannot locate the owner of a sick or injured cat, the doctor can treat, hospitalize, or euthanize the cat without the prior permission of the owner. No liability will attach. Va. Code Ann. §3.1-796.76.

A veterinarian or a staff member may be injured by a cat during the course of its treatment. The cat owner is probably not responsible because the veterinarian and his assistants

Often, a cat is a member of the family. Therefore, find a veterinarian whom you trust.

know and accept the risk of injury. A court may also consider that a doctor's treatment provoked a cat to bite. A doctor has insurance to cover these mishaps. Of course, an owner cannot conceal the fact that his cat is vicious.

If you are unsure or dissatisfied with the veterinarian's recommendations, get a second medical opinion. If a dispute arises, bring in a disinterested third party to mediate. You can lodge a complaint with the state licensing agency or the local veterinary association. The matter can be investigated and disciplinary action taken.

Go to court only as a last resort. Proving that malpractice (legal incompetence or carelessness) caused an injury is a difficult task. Translating the death or injury of a cat into a dollar amount may also be difficult. The cost of a legal battle is likely to be more than the recoverable damages. If a cat died in the doctor's office, the veterinarian may have the burden of proving that malpractice was not a factor.

Landlords, Tenants, and Cats

If a landlord is ambivalent about cats, a well-behaved adult cat is more likely to earn his acceptance than an untrained, mischievous kitten.

Many landlords prefer not to rent to cat owners. A cat can disturb other tenants if it is noisy, messy, smelly, or allowed to wander. Under the right circumstances, any cat can destroy property or injure a person. The cat can cause the landlord a lot of aggravation and expense.

A landlord is permitted to demand that a pet owner take reasonable precautions to control the cat. This is because a landlord who knew of a cat's vicious behavior and could have controlled or removed the animal, but did nothing, could be legally liable for the cat's antics.

Some condominiums or apartments forbid or limit the number of cats that can be kept. An exception may or may not be made for kittens or cats kept temporarily.

Violation of an existing no-pets clause may be a sufficient cause for eviction or the imposition of a penalty. A landlord is entitled to recover the leased property if, after giving the tenant notice to remove a cat under the terms of the rental agreement, the tenant refuses to comply. Or. Rev. Stat. §91.822. The no-cats clause must be reasonable, and the landlord must not have waived his rights. *Longmoor Corporation v. Jeffers*, 205 S.W.2d 234 (Mo. Ct. App. 1947). However, a cat and its owner are entitled to remain on the premises if the rental agreement is not violated. For instance, if the lease stipulates that an eviction must be based on nuisance grounds, the tenant and his pet cannot be removed absent a finding that they are a nuisance, or that eviction is authorized under state or local law. *Hixson v. Leonard*, 186 Misc. 379, 58 N.Y.S.2d 436 (1945).

A no-cats policy may be negotiable. An exception may be made if the prospective tenant can assure the landlord that the cat will not be a problem. But how do you convince the landlord?

There are several things that can be done. Introduce the cat to the landlord. The landlord can see for himself that the cat is well groomed and well mannered. An untrained kitten is not as desirable as a mature, adult cat. A spayed or neutered cat will probably get bonus points. Bring along written

A cat which is well groomed and well behaved may receive a warm
welcome from your prospective landlord.

references from previous landlords and neighbors saying that the cat has not been a problem and is well liked.

Special provisions can be negotiated in private leases that are fair to both sides. A higher rent and a substantial damage deposit may be required. The landlord can define the types of damage and repairs that must be paid by the tenant, both while the tenant lives in the apartment and after he moves out. The lease can limit the number, type, and size of a tenant's cat. Liability insurance may be necessary. The cat may have to remain inside during certain hours.

A rental agreement is a contract that is enforceable for a specific period of time. Its provisions can only be changed by the agreement of both the tenant and the landlord. It cannot be altered unilaterally. Either party is free to renegotiate the terms of the rental contract when it comes up for renewal.

To prevent a landlord from inserting a no-pets clause as an excuse for evicting a tenant with a cat, some states require that any changes in the lease be reasonable. If the cat is a nuisance, the tenant must be given an opportunity to correct the problem before commencement of eviction proceedings. If the cat is not a nuisance, the tenant may argue that the no-pets clause is unreasonable.

A lease may contain a no-pets clause. However, if that clause has not been enforced for a long time, the landlord may have lost his right to object. A landlord may have only a specific period of time to enforce a no-pets clause after finding out about a tenant's pet. The tenant may argue that the no-pets clause is being enforced arbitrarily.

Tenants in public housing are not usually allowed to have cats. Provisions may exist which permit the elderly or persons requiring supportive services to keep domestic cats. Cal. Health & Safety Code §19901. Landlords can include reasonable provisions in the lease. Pet owners are still responsible for damage and injury caused by their cats.

Travel

Laws regarding pet travel may vary from country to country. If you are planning a trip and wish to take along your cat, be sure to consult the appropriate regulating agency well in advance of your departure date.

Some cat owners refuse to go anywhere without their cats. However, most owners do not realize that traveling is stressful for the cat. So if you are not going to leave your cat at home, at least make the trip as comfortable as possible.

Restrictions regarding pet travel are constantly changing due to health and international situations. Therefore, use this discussion only as a guideline. Always contact the appropriate agricultural department or consulate before departing. Give yourself ample time to attend to the documentation and allow for postal delays. Arrangements have to be made with your veterinarian for an examination shortly before your pet's departure.

Of course, your cat should be properly identified. The cat's name, and your name, address, and telephone number should be attached to the cat at all times. Most states and countries require a recent health certificate.

IMPORTING AND EXPORTING

Into the U.S.

The Animal Welfare Act mandates the requirements for importing birds and animals into the U.S. The Department of Agriculture is responsible for setting the standards regarding the care, transportation, handling, and treatment of cats. The importing conditions must be humane and healthy.

Each container of cats imported must be plainly marked, labeled, or tagged on the outside with the names and addresses of the shipper and the consignee. 9 C.F.R. §3.11. An accurate invoice statement specifying the number of each species contained in the shipment must also be included.

The U.S. Department of Health and Human Services regulates the quarantine program. The guidelines are set out in 42 C.F.R., part 71. The purpose of this rule is to prevent the introduction, transmission, and spread of communicable diseases from foreign countries into the United States. 42 C.F.R. §71.1.

You must comply with all restrictions before introducing your pet to a foreign country.

The regulations stipulate that pets brought into the country be examined at the first port of entry for any evidence of disease communicable to humans. A cat that does not appear to be in good health may be confined. The pet owner bears the expense of examination, tests, and treatment. A cat that is barred from entering the U.S. can be exported or destroyed. 42 C.F.R. §71.51(b).

Cats are not subject to a mandatory quarantine period (except in Hawaii), nor do they require a health certificate or rabies vaccination. Usually, cats also travel free of duty.

Since the hours of service and the availability of inspectors vary from port to port, check with your anticipated port of arrival prior to importation. This will reduce the possibility of unnecessary delay.

Direct further inquiries to your local customs office or the following agencies:

Dept. of Health and Human Services
Center for Disease Control
Division of Quarantine
Atlanta, GA 30333
(404) 639-2574

Animal and Plant Health Inspection Service
U.S. Dept. of Agriculture
Hyattsville, MD 20782
(301) 436-7786

Dept. of the Treasury
U.S. Customs Service
Washington, D.C. 20229

Into Foreign Countries

When leaving the U.S., call or write the country into which you want to take your pet, or contact the respective embassy in Washington, D.C., or the nearest consulate office, to find out requirements for entry. The movement of cats from one country to another is strictly controlled by the

Some cats are calmer than others, and these are the ones that can weather an extended trip quite well.

government of each country. Failure to adhere to the regulations may result in fines, re-export, or even the destruction of the cat. You can comply with the requirements yourself, or you can engage the services of a company which specializes in animal transport.

All cats entering the United Kingdom and Ireland are required to be vaccinated against rabies and to complete a six-month quarantine period at an approved station. The normal minimum requirements for mainland Europe and Canada include a health certificate issued within 48 hours prior to exportation, a rabies vaccination certificate, and an export certificate from the country of residence of the cat. Prior permission to export to Australia is required, as well as completion of a quarantine period.

Crossing State Boundaries

Regulations pertaining to preventing the interstate spread of communicable diseases are contained in 21 C.F.R., parts 1240 and 1250.

If you plan to ship your cat by common carrier across state lines, contact the importing state beforehand to learn about regulations regarding crating, inoculations, health certificates, and costs.

The ASPCA publishes a booklet "Traveling With Your Pet." It includes travel tips, interstate travel requirements, and importation requirements for the United States, as well as for many foreign countries. For your copy contact:.

ASPCA Education Department
441 East 92nd Street
New York, NY 10128
(212) 876-7700 ext. 3412

Hawaii

All cats entering the State of Hawaii are subject to requirements in addition to those mentioned already for the Department of Health and Human Services. All cats must

107

Transport enclosures must conform to the legal standards.

complete a 120-day quarantine period at the State Animal Quarantine Station in Oahu.

There is no discretionary authority to waive or shorten the quarantine for cats except for cats originating in Australia, New Zealand, and the United Kingdom.

You can ship your cat ahead of your arrival. The airline will deliver your pet to the Animal Holding Facility. The State of Hawaii will provide all the necessary transportation. The payment of fees by the owner is due at the time the cat enters quarantine.

You can visit your pet at the facility, or you can designate a friend or relative to watch over your cat. The quarantine station will gladly provide you with a list of groomers and sponsors willing to visit, bathe, groom, and otherwise care for a cat whose owner is not on the island.

The health of the cat while it is quarantined is the responsibility of the owner. The quarantine station is not equipped with hospital facilities or supplies for major medical problems.

For additional information, call or write the:
State of Hawaii
Dept. of Agriculture
Division of Animal Industry
99-762 Moanalua Road
Aiea, HI 96701-3246
(808) 488-8462

TRANSPORT STANDARDS OF COMMERCIAL CARRIERS AND INTERMEDIATE HANDLERS

The Animal Welfare Act protects cats and other animals traveling in commerce. Motor vehicles, airplanes, railroads, and ships must comply with the act. These federal regulations require carriers and intermediate handlers to refuse to transport an animal unless the following criteria are met.

Although the requirements are similar, each airline has its own particular regulations. Check with your carrier before flying.

The cat must be 1) at least eight weeks old; 2) certified as healthy within ten days prior to departure; 3) secured in a carrier which meets the standards, 9 C.F.R. §3.12; and 4) adequately identified. 9 C.F.R. §3.11.

Primary enclosures used to transport cats must be sturdy and well ventilated. They should be large enough to allow the cat to stand, turn around, and lie down comfortably. The carrier must be marked "Live Animals." Documents must be attached in an easily accessible manner to the outside of the enclosure. A clean, soft, absorbent litter material which is safe and non-toxic to animals should be included. 9 C.F.R. §3.12. Shipping crates can be purchased at the airport.

Your name, address, and phone number, the cat's name, its destination, and food and water requirements should be on the outside of the container. A favorite toy and an article of clothing with your scent on it make travel more comfortable. Attach a gravity-flow water bottle in such a way that it can be refilled without having to open the cage. Do not medicate your cat without consulting a veterinarian.

Carriers and intermediate handlers shall provide water at least every 12 hours after acceptance for shipment. Cats over 16 weeks old shall be fed at least once every 24 hours. Kittens less than 16 weeks old shall have food at least every 12 hours. 9 C.F.R. §3.14. The cats must be observed at least every four hours. 9 C.F.R. §3.15. The primary enclosure must be handled in a manner that avoids physical and emotional trauma. It must be protected from sunlight, rain, snow, and cold weather. 9 C.F.R. §3.17.

AIRLINES

A cat can be brought into the cabin as carry-on baggage, or it can be checked into the cargo section. Although the guidelines are similar, each airline has its own restrictions, so call the particular airline in advance.

An uncontrolled cat is a hazard in a moving vehicle.

Generally, a cat allowed in the cabin as carry-on must be in a carrier small enough to fit under the seat. The number of animals permitted on a flight may be limited to one, or it may be determined by the time of year and the type of aircraft. There may also be a restriction as to the number of carriers allowed per passenger. A reservation is required, and there is usually a fee.

Due to the size restriction of carry-on baggage, some carriers must be stored in the cargo section. Here there is usually no size restriction, but all other restrictions apply. The weight of the cat and carrier will probably have to be 100 pounds or less. Heavier weights must be checked as air freight. This is more expensive due to the use of the equipment involved to move the enclosure.

There is a chance that your cat may be injured during its journey. The airlines restrict their financial liability to a certain amount regardless of the actual value of your loss. If you want extra coverage, you must declare a higher value for your "baggage" and pay an additional fee. Extra coverage can also be purchased from a private insurer. Since most problems occur on the ground and not during flight time, try to book non-stop flights. Confirm with flight attendants and baggage carriers that your cat is on board.

MOTOR VEHICLE, RAIL, AIR AND MARINE CARRIERS

The animal cargo space of these carriers must be designed, constructed, and maintained to protect the health and ensure the safety and comfort of a cat. 9 C.F.R. §3.13.

Many public transportation vehicles do not allow cats at all. Some permit cats if they are secured in a carrier. Contact the particular bus, train, air, or boat line to learn its policy. If cats are allowed, inspect the area if it is separate from where you will be. It should be safe, clean, and well ventilated.

CARS

Many cats are accustomed to traveling short distances in a car. However, no pet should be permitted to ride in the front seat, hang out the window, or jump around. A cat must be taught to settle down in the back seat. If your cat is undisciplined, then it must be restrained in a carrier. An uncontrolled cat is a hazard in a moving car.

When traveling long distances, periodically allow the cat to exercise and relieve itself. Never leave a cat unattended in the car. It takes only minutes for a car to heat up in the summer and to cool down in the winter. Some states have laws against leaving a cat alone in a car. Such poor conduct may violate anti-cruelty laws.

ACCOMMODATIONS

Animalports

At least two airports provide special services for animals. JFK Airport in New York has a facility run by the ASPCA. It services both JFK and LaGuardia airports. The Animal-Port–Houston is a registered Texas corporation. It has facilities at both the Hobby and Intercontinental airports. The animalports are accessible 24 hours a day, 365 days a year.

A cat can be boarded at an animalport while its owner is away. In addition, the personnel will assist pet owners, shippers, and airlines in handling animals that are being transported. Traveling crates are available for purchase. Cats traveling alone can spend their layover time at the stress-relieving accommodations. The staff feeds, waters, exercises, and otherwise cares for the residents. Veterinarians are on call. Current vaccinations are required.

A cat may be brought to the JFK Animalport for boarding, or arrangements can be made for pick-up or drop-off service at JFK or LaGuardia airports. For further information, contact the

ASCPA Animalport
JFK International Airport
Air Cargo Building 189
Jamaica, NY 11430
(718) 656-6042
Fax: 718-656-6051
Cable: ANIMALPORT

The Animal-Port-Houston will pick up or drop off the cat at your home. Transportation is also available to take your pet anywhere in Houston, such as to the veterinarian, trainer, or groomer. A staff member will even accompany your cat on its flight if you request.

Direct further inquiries:

Animal-Port–Houston
P.O. Box 60564 AMF
Houston, TX 77205
(713) 821-2244
FAX: 713–821-1128

Hotels and Motels

Many hotels and motels do not allow cats. Therefore, it is wise to call in advance, or you might find yourself without a place to stay.

Kennels

You may prefer to board your pet. Do not take a chance on just any kennel or cattery, though. Your cat deserves reliable accommodations. Inspect any temporary home for your pet.

Cruelty

Due to the concerted efforts of various animal rights groups, the general public is becoming increasingly aware of what constitutes humane—and inhumane—treatment of cats, as well as many other kinds of animals.

Most jurisdictions have enacted laws which forbid cruelty to animals. Inhumane treatment may include intentional abuse, neglect, theft, and abandonment whereby unjustifiable pain or suffering results. Failure to provide food, water, shelter, or protection, leaving a cat which was injured by your car, confining a cat in a parked car in a manner which endangers its health or safety, Md. Transp. Code Ann. §21-1004.1, and poor conditions in a pet shop may all be considered cruelty.

Not every act or omission to act is prohibited. In some places, it is lawful to kill a cat in the act of seriously injuring a person or damaging property. In addition, millions of unclaimed cats are killed each year by animal shelters. However, a cat killed by a veterinarian, a pound, or a dealer must be destroyed in a manner that causes as little pain as possible.

If you suspect improper behavior, first talk to the owner. If the maltreatment does not cease, report the abuse to the humane society, the police, a local animal society, and anyone else you think has the right to take action. It is best to have the complaint in writing. Keep a copy for yourself.

Except in the case of an emergency, the cat owner is entitled to notice before the cat can be taken away. A mistreated cat can be seized by the authorities and impounded. If the cruelty is particularly outrageous, the abuser may be subject to a fine or a jail sentence. The owner may also have to pay for the cost of impoundment before he can get the cat back.

RESEARCH

The number of cats and other animals used for scientific research is estimated to be in the millions. Using cats for scientific research is usually not punishable by law. The pain and suffering inflicted on live animals for research are considered justifiable. The experimentation has practical medical benefits, such as advancing the study of cancer, diabetes, alcoholism, heart disease, infectious diseases, drugs, and surgical treatments.

Hence, a researcher at an institute conducting medical and scientific experiments on live monkeys did not violate a state statute prohibiting cruelty to animals. The statute was held to be inapplicable to activities in which the pain inflicted on an animal was incidental and unavoidable. *Taub v. State*, 296 Md. 439, 463 A.2d 819, 42 A.L.R.4th 853 (1983). Furthermore, a state statute forbidding cruelty to animals was not violated when classroom experiments were conducted on live chickens. The experiment was determined to have scientific and educational value, and was conducted under the supervision of certified instructors. *N.J.S.P.C.A. v. Bd. of Educ. of East Orange*, 91 N.J.Super 81, 219 A.2d 200, affd 49 N.J. 15, 227 A.2d 506 (1966). Some jurisdictions outlaw experiments on live animals in schools for purposes of demonstration. Ill. Ann. Stat. ch. 122, §27-14.

There are about 7,000 animal rights groups in the United States. They question the moral justification for sacrificing animals for the benefit of mankind. Their demands range from securing better lab conditions to setting all the animals free.

The troubling conditions at respected research centers has improved over the years. The number of animals used in experimentation has declined as other research methods have been developed. The conditions of care in the research facilities have changed for the better.

Research facilities are regulated by federal laws which require that humane care and treatment be provided. Each research facility must obtain a federal registration. 9 C.F.R. §2.25. It must conform to the standards, 9 C.F.R. §2.26, and record keeping requirements, 9 C.F.R. §2.76, of the Animal Welfare Act. Proposed amendments to the act require improved laboratory conditions. The changes call for a reduction in the number of animals sacrificed, the refinement of techniques that cause suffering, and the replacement of live animals with simulations or cell cultures where possible. A national data bank will list the results of all animal experiments so that repetition will be minimized. Laboratories must set up animal-care committees, submit to regular inspections, provide larger cages, and allow the animals to exercise and socialize regularly.

Some institutions have implemented their own reforms without waiting for legal compulsion. They keep the animals mentally and emotionally stimulated by providing games and activities. Some firms have pledged to halt animal tests as soon as alternatives are available. A few cosmetics companies have discontinued using animals in their product testing.

The moral debate rages on, though. Some scientists consider the reforms excessive, while animal rights activists claim that the reforms are too modest.

Handling a Controversy

If the actions of a cat are a point of contention between the cat's owner and his neighbor, a calm and reasonable dialogue can be more beneficial than an acrimonious shouting match.

A cat can be predatory, or it can be just a nuisance. Either way, if you have a cat like this in your neighborhood, or if you are the owner of the cat, you may have to handle a dispute. Your cat may have caused damage or injury, or it may be the victim. Either way, you must be prepared to manage the encounter in a reasonable, responsible, and legally acceptable manner.

A CAT ATTACK

A cat attack is an unlikely occurrence; however, it is possible that you may be a victim of, or a witness to, an attack. There are a variety of things you can do to prevent or stop an attack. Most states permit you to take any steps that are reasonably necessary under the circumstances, including killing the cat.

Most cat attacks happen quickly. The event is often over in a matter of seconds because a cat does not usually remain engaged in battle; it merely bites or scratches, then releases.

Get the name and address of the cat and its owner. If that is not possible, write down an accurate description of the cat. This way the cat can be identified at a later time. If the cat is not tagged, the authorities may be able to capture the cat for quarantine. This is to determine if the cat is rabid.

Get the names and addresses of all other people, including children, who witnessed the event. Write a short summary of the incident. Memories are short, but a written document lasts a long time.

If a person is injured, get medical attention immediately. A bite or scratch may require medication. A bump or swelling may indicate a sprain or break. All medical bills, including x-rays, therapy, and prescriptions, should be kept as evidence of treatment.

The event should be reported to the local animal control department. This way the cat's vicious tendencies will be on record. If the cat attacks again, it will be on record that the owner had notice of the cat's propensity to cause harm.

The cat's owner should be notified of the incident. Explain to the owner what happened. It may be best to put this in writing, including a detailed account of the injury and expenses. Assess the damage and negotiate with the owner for a settlement. Ask for a reasonable amount. Often an owner is willing to cover the cost of the injury. Handling the situation directly with the owner is more expedient than going through insurance companies or the legal system.

Tell the owner that his homeowner's or renter's insurance may cover the event. Many cat owners do not know this. Set a date for payment. Referring to the local law may be persuasive. If an agreement is worked out, put it in writing. This protects you, as well as the owner, if there is a disagreement later.

If the damage is extensive, or the owner is unwilling to accept responsibility, only then should you consider getting an attorney. Utilizing the legal system can be expensive, time consuming, and nerve wracking. If a lot of money is not involved (less than a couple of thousand dollars), a less costly alternative is to go to small claims court.

A NUISANCE PROBLEM

A cat may not be dangerous, but it can be a nuisance. Some irksome antics include digging up your yard, scattering your garbage across the lawn, ravaging your prized garden, crying incessantly or late at night, and scaring you or your kids.

If you are the aggrieved neighbor, the first thing to do is to talk to the cat's owner. Use a reasonable and friendly approach—avoid animosity. An owner will probably be more eager to please a neighbor that does not have a threatening manner. You would be surprised at how many owners do not realize that their cat is disturbing you. Maybe they do not know that their cat is ravaging your garbage cans. A cat owner is usually apologetic and willing to take the necessary steps to control the cat. Maybe you can offer some suggestions as to how to remedy the situation, such as keeping the cat indoors after dark, or calling the humane society for advice.

If the cat stops its annoying behavior, take the time to thank the owner. Obviously he took your complaint seriously, so he should know that his corrective measures worked.

If you happen to be the owner of the cat wreaking havoc, be understanding, not hostile. After all, you are responsible for keeping your cat from annoying your neighbors. Additionally, your neighbor has probably had several encounters with your cat before he came to talk to you. Take the proper measures to stop the cat's poor behavior. After a few days, visit your neighbor to be sure the problem has been solved.

If talking to your neighbor is a dead-end, try mediation. This method of settling disputes outside of a courtroom involves the imposition of a neutral third party. This individual acts as a link between the disputing parties to keep the lines of communication open. A mediator is not to choose sides; he merely identifies problems and suggests compromises.

Some communities have professional or volunteer dispute resolution services. Look in the yellow pages, or call your local court house, bar association, chamber of commerce, or police department. Or, a mediator can be a neutral friend or neighbor who is respected by both parties.

Once the differences are settled, define the terms in a writing signed by both parties.

ANIMAL CONTROL AUTHORITIES

There may be a reason you do not want to talk to your neighbor, or talking to him was a disaster, or maybe you just do not know who owns the troublesome cat. Call your local police, animal control department, or health or public safety

A judge will probably be more receptive to someone who has tried to settle a dispute before coming to court.

authorities. The people responsible for controlling cats can call or visit the cat owner, issue a citation, or even make an arrest.

These departments may have guidelines to follow. For example, a certain number of complaints may have to be registered before action can be taken. So do not just call and complain. Find out the procedures and follow through with them. Look up all the pertinent local law, such as ordinances dealing with noise, nuisances, cats roaming at large, personal injury, property damage, or the number of cats allowed per household, and have it enforced. Enlist the aid of other neighbors who are annoyed. Most importantly, be persistent.

SMALL CLAIMS COURT

In small claims court, an attorney is not needed and the wait to get before a judge may be as little as a few weeks. Many states have free publications describing the procedures required in their small claims court. A few courts even have advisors to answer questions.

Familiarize yourself with the law so that you can make sure your complaint meets all the required elements. Good preparation is vital to presenting a sound argument. Be brief and articulate, not boring. Present your case in an organized manner. You may be allowed to present witnesses and to utilize documents, police reports, hospital records, medical bills, and photographs. Avoid confusion and repetition. But most importantly, always be respectful to both the judge and your adversary.

Even small claims court imposes some requirements. First, check the jurisdictional limit; small claims court usually restricts the amount to under a couple of thousand dollars. Listed below are the small claims court awards limits for each state.

Second, be sure your complaint is not barred by the statute of limitations; each court has a limited amount of time, as measured from the date of the event, in which you can bring suit. Fortunately, if the annoyance is an on-going event, there is no limit to the number of suits that can be brought. Therefore, subsequent events are not barred if a timely suit is commenced.

Third, small claims court restricts your award to money damages; you cannot get an injunction—a court order instructing the cat owner to do or not to do something. However, the number of suits that can be brought is unlimited. Paying damage awards can get expensive and may influence the cat owner to take remedial action.

Fourth, the amount of money recoverable in small claims court may be restricted to actual out-of-pocket expenses; compensation for pain and suffering may be barred.

Fifth, attempt to work things out with your neighbor before going to court. Even if not required by law, a judge will probably be more receptive to someone who shows a good faith effort to resolve the dispute out of court.

State	Citation	Dollar Amount
Alabama	Ala. Code §12-12-31	1000
Alaska	Alaska Stat. §22.15.040	5000★★
Arizona	Ariz. Rev. Stat. Ann. §22-201	500
Arkansas	Ark. Code Ann. §16-17-704	3000
California	Cal. Civ. Proc. Code §116.2	2000 2500 eff. 1/1/91
Colorado	Colo. Rev. Stat. Ann. §13-6-403	2600★
Connecticut	Conn. Gen. Stat. Ann. §51-15	1500
Delaware	Unavailable	
District of Columbia	D.C. Code Ann. §11-1321	2000★
Florida	Fla. Stat. Ann. §34.01	5000★
Georgia	Ga. Code Ann. art. 6 §3	200
Hawaii	Hawaii Rev. Stat. §633-27	2500★
Idaho	Idaho Code §1-2301	2000★
Illinois	Ill. Ann. Stat. ch. 110A §281	2500
Indiana	Ind. Code Ann §33-11/6-4-21	3000★
Iowa	Iowa Code Ann. §631.1	2000★

Kansas	Kan. Stat. Ann. §61-2703	1000
Kentucky	Ky. Rev. Stat. Ann. §24A:230	1500★
Louisiana	La. Rev. Stat. Ann. §13:5202	2000★
Maine	Me. Rev. Stat. Ann. tit. 14§7482	1400★
Maryland	Md. Ann. Code §4-405	2500★
Massachusetts	Mass. Gen. Laws Ann. Ch. 21 §21	1500
Michigan	Mich. Comp. Laws Ann. §600.6419	1000★
Minnesota	Minn. Stat. Ann. §488.04	1000
Mississippi	Miss. Code Ann. §9-11-9	1000
Missouri	Mo. Ann. Stat. §482.305	1500★
Montana	Mont. Code Ann. §25-34-102	1500
Nebraska	Neb. Rev. Stat. §2654-522	1500★
Nevada	Nev. Rev. Stat. Ann. §73.010	1500
New Hampshire	N.H. Rev. Stat. Ann. §503.1	1500★
New Jersey	N.J. Stat. Ann. §2A:6-43	1000★
New Mexico	N.M. Stat. Ann. §34-8A-3	5000
New York	N.Y. Judiciary-Court Acts Law	2000★
North Carolina	N.C. Gen. Stat. Ann. §7A-210	1500
North Dakota	N.D. Cent. Code Ann. §27-08.1-01	2000
Ohio	Ohio Rev. Code Ann. §1925.02	1000★
Oklahoma	Okla. Stat. Ann. tit. 12 §1754	1500
Oregon	Or. Rev. Stat. §46.405	200
Pennsylvania	Pa. Cons. Stat. Ann. tit. 42 §1123	5000★
Puerto Rico	Laws of P.R. Ann. T.32APPIII Rule 6	500
Rhode Island	R.I. Gen. Laws §10-16-1	1500
South Carolina	S.C. Code Ann. §22-3-10	2500
South Dakota	S.D. Codified Laws §15-39-45	2000★
Tennessee	Unavailable	
Texas	Tex. Civ. Code Ann. §28.003	1000
Utah	Utah Code Ann. §78-6-1	1000★
Vermont	Vt. Stat. Ann. tit. 12 §5531	2000★
Virginia	Va. Code Ann. §16-1-122.2	1000★
Washington	Wash. Rev. Code Ann. §12:40.010	2000
West Virginia	Unavailable	
Wisconsin	Wis. Stat. Ann. §799.01(4)	2000
Wyoming	Wyo. Stat. Ann. §1-21-201	2000

★Excludes costs and interest.
★★Excludes costs, interests, and attorney fees.

The Animal Welfare Act

THE ANIMAL WELFARE ACT

The Animal Welfare Act regulates the humane handling, care, treatment, and transport of animals used for research or exhibition, sold as pets, or transported in commerce. The statement of policy sets forth that it is necessary to regulate animals and activities in order: 1) to insure that animals intended for use in research facilities or for exhibition purposes or for use as pets are provided humane care and treatment; 2) to assure the humane treatment of animals during transportation in commerce; and 3) to protect the owners of animals from the theft of their animals by preventing the sale or use of animals which have been stolen. 7 U.S.C. §2131.

The standards and regulations govern animal dealers, exhibitors, operators of auction sales, carriers, and intermediate handlers. Expressed are minimum requirements with respect to handling, housing, feeding, sanitation, veterinary care, and other matters. The present version of the Animal Welfare Act can be found at 9 C.F.R., parts 1, 2, and 3. A short synopsis of the authority of the government under the act is presented here.

Any person operating or desiring to operate as a dealer, exhibitor, or operator of an auction sale must demonstrate that his premises and equipment comply with the standards. 9 C.F.R. §2.3. A licensee must file a report each year describing his business. 9 C.F.R. §2.7. Research facilities must also file a report showing that professionally acceptable standards governed the care, treatment, and use of animals. 9 C.F.R. §2.28

Every dealer and exhibitor, 9 C.F.R. §2.75, research facility, 9 C.F.R. §2.76, and carrier and intermediate handler, 9 C.F.R. §2.78, must maintain a system of records that discloses detailed information about each cat in its possession or under its control. The records must be maintained for at least one year. 9 C.F.R. §2.81. All records, facilities, and animals are subject to inspection by government officials who have the authority to enforce provisions of the act. 9 C.F.R. §2.126.

Enclosures must allow a cat to stand up and turn around.

No dealer, research facility, exhibitor, operator of an auction sale, or department, agency, or instrumentality of the United States or of any state or local government shall deliver to any intermediate handler or carrier for transportation, in commerce, any cat unaccompanied by a health certificate issued by a licensed veterinarian. The veterinarian must have inspected the cat within ten days of transport. The document must certify that the animal appeared to be free of any infectious disease or physical abnormality which would endanger the animal or the public health. 9 C.F.R. §2.79.

PROPOSED CHANGES TO THE ANIMAL WELFARE ACT

Proposed revisions and amendments to 9 C.F.R., parts 1, 2, and 3, have been published in the Federal Register/Vol. 54, No. 49/Wednesday, March 15, 1989. These federal proposals concern dealers, exhibitors, research facilities, and transporters. Private owners are not affected. These rules are important because, if accepted, they are likely to be incorporated into state statutes and local ordinances. Some of the revisions are summarized below.

Humidity 9 C.F.R. §3.2(b)

Indoor facilities housing cats will have a new humidity standard. The humidity must be maintained between 30 and 70 percent.

Enclosures 9 C.F.R. §3.6(b)

Enclosures for cats will be increased. Floor space requirements will be based on the weight of the cat. Every queen with nursing kittens will be provided with an additional amount of floor space. The minimum floor space would be exclusive of any food, water, or litter pans. The height of the enclosure would have to be at least 24 inches (60.96 cm.).

The law sets food and water requirements for transport.

All cats in the same primary enclosure would have to be compatible. No more than 12 adult unconditioned cats could be housed together. Additionally, queens in heat could not be housed with sexually mature males, except for breeding purposes. Queens with kittens less than four months old could not be housed with any other adult cats, except if maintained in a breeding colony. Cats with vicious dispositions would have to be housed individually.

Resting surfaces would not be counted as part of the minimum floor space. The areas would have to be elevated and impervious to moisture. Additionally, they would either have to be easily cleaned and sanitized or easily replaceable when soiled or worn.

Feeding   9 C.F.R. §3.8(a)

Food given to a cat must be appropriate for the animal's age. Food receptacles must be sanitized regularly. Measures must be taken to prevent molding, deterioration, and caking of food.

Cleaning of Primary Enclosures 9 C.F.R. §3.10(a)

Excreta and food waste must be removed at least daily and as often as necessary.

Transport 9 C.F.R. §3.13

Written instructions concerning food and water requirements for each cat in the shipment must be securely attached to the outside of the primary enclosure before a carrier or handler can accept it for transport. A carrier or handler cannot accept a cat for shipment unless there is a certification specifying the date and time each cat was last provided food and water.

Transport Enclosures 9 C.F.R. §3.14

Containers would need to have ventilation on each of the four walls. The openings must be at least eight percent of the total surface of each wall.

Pet shops sell a variety of carrying cases which are easily cleaned, well ventilated, and sturdy.

Kittens less than 180 days old could not be transported in the same enclosure with adult cats other than their dams. Aggressive cats must be transported individually. Female cats in season must not be transported in the same primary enclosure with any male cat.

When shipped by air, no more than two live cats, six months old or more, comparable in size, and over 20 pounds each, could be transported in the same enclosure. A maximum of three live kittens, eight weeks to six months of age, weighing less than 20 pounds (9kg) each, can be shipped in the same primary enclosure. When shipped by land, a maximum of four cats may be transported in the same enclosure, provided that all other transportation requirements are met.

Transport Temperatures 9 C.F.R. §3.14(f)

The temperatures to which a cat is exposed during transport must meet generally accepted temperature ranges for the age, condition, and breed of the animal.

Food and Water During Transport 9 C.F.R. §3.16

Consignors would be required to provide water within four hours and food within 12 hours before delivery for transport. The time periods for providing food and water to the animals after acceptance for transport begin at the time the cat was last provided food and water.

Additional Requirements for Research Facilities 9 C.F.R. §2.30

Research facilities must ensure that adequate veterinary care, including the appropriate use of drugs or euthanasia, is provided for at all times. Pain and distress must be minimized. The attending veterinarian has the authority to inspect all animal areas at any time.

When performing procedures which might reasonably be expected to be painful, the research facility must give assura-

Cats are used for experimental as well as instructional purposes in schools.

nce that alternative procedures were considered, but were not suitable. The chosen experiment must not unnecessarily duplicate previous experiments.

Pain-relieving drugs, anesthetics, analgesics, and tranquilizers must be used to minimize pain. They are to be withheld only as long as necessary, and only if scientifically necessary, fully explained, and justified.

The research facility shall establish a reporting procedure whereby personnel or employees can report problems, deviations, and deficiencies.

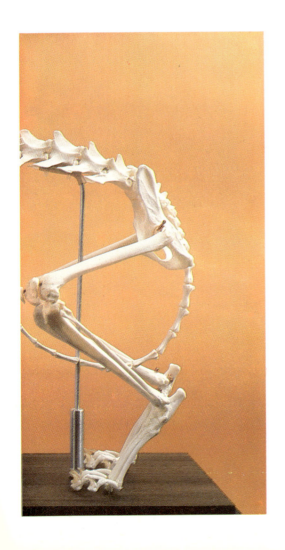

Cat Laws

Laws dealing with cats can be found at the federal and state level, but for the most part, cat law is a local matter.

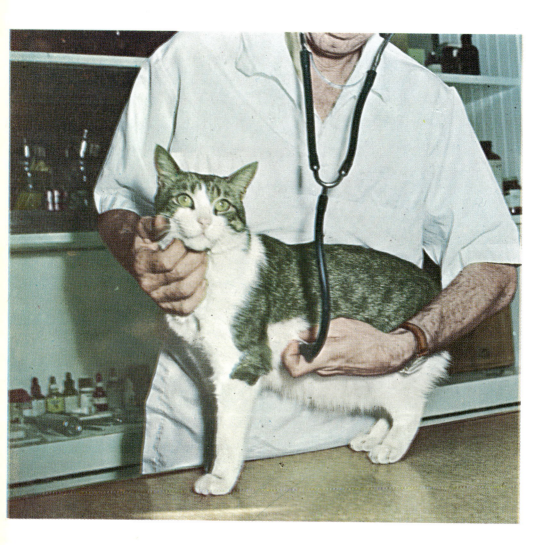

The law requires that, if a cat has to be euthanized, the procedure must be done in a humane manner.

Listed below is a sampling of the law pertaining to cats. Not all of the cat statutes are included. The statutes are listed under an assortment of titles, including cats, pets, agriculture, animals, nuisance, etc. The cat related topics covered by statutes and ordinances vary widely from jurisdiction to jurisdiction and change over time.

Alabama
Ala. Code

§3-7-1	Definitions.
§3-7-2	Requirements as to inoculation of animals generally; quarantine and inoculation of exotic and wildlife pets; sale or offer for sale, etc., of antirabies vaccine to persons other than rabies inspectors or licensed veterinarians.
§3-7-3	Inoculation fee.
§3-7-4	Tags—Issuance; contents; wearing requirement.
§3-7-5	Same—Replacement of lost tags.
§3-7-6	Same—Penalty when animal found without tag.
§3-7-7	Impounding of animals running at large in violation of chapter—Authorized facilities for impoundment; notice to owner of impounded animal.
§3-7-8	Same—Redemption of impounded animals; disposition of unclaimed animals.
§3-7-9	Confinement of animals which have bitten humans; failure of person having knowledge of person having been bitten to report same, etc.; liability of owner of confined animal for handling expenses; when biting animals may be destroyed and head submitted for examination.
§3-7-10	Rabies inspectors.
§3-7-11	Penalty for violations of chapter, etc.
§3-7-12	Quarantining of areas of state, etc., to prevent spread of rabies.
§3-7-13	Effect of chapter on municipalities.

Some shelters donate unclaimed cats for research.

Arizona
Ariz. Rev. Stat. Ann.

§24-371	Establishment of county pounds; impounding and disposing of dogs and cats; reclaiming impounded dogs and cats; pound fees.
§24-372	Handling of biting animals; responsibility for reporting animal bites; authority to destroy animals.

Arkansas
Ark. Stat. Ann.

§20-19-103	Sterilization of impounded dogs and cats.
§20-19-201	Municipal ordinances unaffected.
§20-19-202	Vaccination required.
§20-19-203	Administration.
§20-19-302	Definitions.
§20-19-303	Power of political subdivisions not limited—applicability.
§20-19-304	Penalties.
§20-19-305	Vaccination for dogs and cats required.
§20-19-306	Illegal acts when person bitten.
§20-19-307	Confinement of animal when person bitten.
§20-19-308	Shipment of head of animal suspected of being rabid to laboratory.
§20-19-309	Area quarantine.
§20-19-310	Authority to impose additional measures.

California
Cal. Civ. Code

§1834.5	Abandoned animals; disposition; notice.
§1834.6	Use of abandoned animals for scientific or other experimentation prohibited.
§1834.7	Use of animals turned in to shelter for research; sign on pound or animal regulation department.

Cal. Food & Agric.

§31751.5	Spayed or neutered cats; reduction in fee.
§31751.6	Licensed cattery; exemption from tag requirement.

The law prohibits a person from injuring, taking, or destroying someone else's property. This includes furniture, as well as cats . . . since a cat is property.

§31752   Impounded cats; period of holding before killing.

Cal. Health & Safety
§19901   Public housing for the elderly or persons requiring supportive services; pets.

Connecticut
Conn. Gen. Stat. Ann.

§22-329   Prevention of cruelty to dogs and other animals.

§22-344   Licensing of commercial kennel, pet shop, training facility or grooming facility. Fees. Inspection. Conformance to zoning regulations.

§22-369   Unknown owners; notice.
§22-374   Animals at large; impounding; notice.
§22-377   Trespasser's act; proceedings; penalty.
§22-380a   Spaying and neutering clinics established. Fees.

§22-380b   Procedure for spaying and neutering.
§22-380c   Receipt and disposition of funds. Program termination.

District of Columbia
D.C. Code Ann.

§6-1001   Definitions.
§6-1002   Animal Control Agency.
§6-1003   Vaccinations.
§6-1004   Licenses and fees.
§6-1005   Impoundment.
§6-1006   Release to owner.
§6-1007   Adoption.
§6-1008   Prohibited conduct.
§6-1009   Animal hobby permit.
§6-1010   Education and incentive program.
§6-1013   Notice of violation.

The claws and teeth of a cat can do extensive damage.

Florida
Fla. Stat. Ann.

§585.195	Dogs and cats transported or offered for sale; health requirements.
§823.04	Diseased animals.
§823.041	Disposal of bodies of dead animals; penalty.
§828.02	Definition of animal.
§828.03	Agents of counties, societies, etc., may prosecute violators.
§828.05	Killing an injured or diseased domestic animal.
§828.055	Sodium pentobarbital; permits for use in euthanasia of domestic animals.
§828.058	Euthanasia of dogs and cats.
§828.073	Animals found in distress; when agent may take charge; hearing; disposition; sale.
§828.12	Cruelty to animals.
§828.122	Fighting or baiting animals; offenses; penalties.
§828.13	Confinement of animals without sufficient food, water, or exercise; abandonment of animals.
§828.27	Local animal control or cruelty ordinances; penalty.

Georgia
Ga. Code Ann.

§44-1-8	Property rights in animals, etc., generally; factors establishing property in wild animals.
§51-2-7	Liability of owner or keeper of vicious or dangerous animal for injuries caused by animal.

Idaho
Idaho Code

§18-5803	Exposure of animal carcasses.

Wildlife is property. If your cat attacks a wild creature, you may be responsible.

Illinois
Ill. Ann. Stat. ch. 8

§302	Definitions.
§352	Owner.
§363	Report of bite by dog or other animal—Confinement—Report—Notification by administrator—Report at end of confinement—Confinement in owner's house—Reduction of period—Violations—Expense.
§364	Prevention of spread of rabies—Powers.
§365	Enclosure or run line for vicious dog—Leash for dangerous dog or other animal—Exemptions—Injunction—Nuisance.

ch. 111½

§129	License—Institutions requiring live dogs or cats for scientific or educational activities.

ch. 122

§27-14	Experiments upon animals.

Indiana
Ind. Code Ann.

§15-2.1-21-8	Running at large.
§15-2.1-21-9	Violations.
§15-2.1-21-14	Penalty; civil action; injunctions.

Kansas
Kan. Stat. Ann.

§47-1720	Research facility license.
§47-1731	Dogs and cats; spaying or neutering required, when.

Kentucky
Ky. Rev. Stat. Ann.

§257.160	Disposition of carcasses—How and when made.
§258.060	Physicians to report persons bitten by and other animals.

Maine
Me. Rev. Stat. Ann. tit 7,

§1809	Permits for state entry.

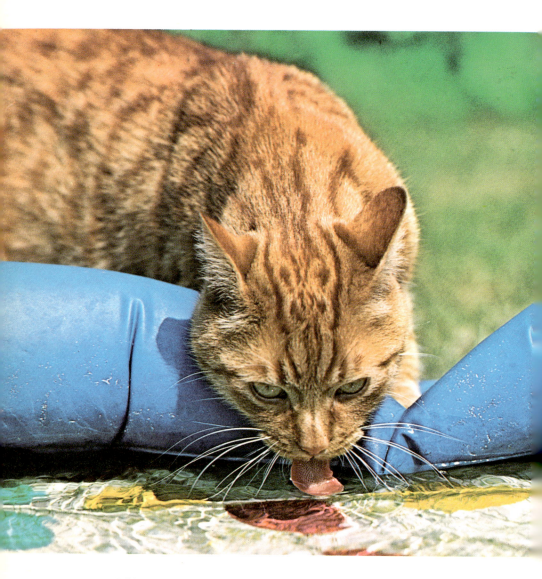

Your neighbor has added toxic chemicals to his swimming pool to control algae and mosquitoes. Your cat drank from the pool and was poisoned. Who is responsible? You, your neighbor, or the manufacturer of the chemicals? . . . It may be any or all of these people.

Maryland
Md. Transp. Code Ann.

§21-1004.1	Cats or dogs left in standing or parked vehicle.

Massachusetts
Mass. Gen. Laws Ann.

ch. 140

§138A	Importation of dogs and cats for commercial resale; health certificates; violations.
§139A	Shelters; sale or gift of dog or cat not spayed or neutered.

ch. 272

§77	Cruelty to animals.

Michigan
Mich. Comp. Laws Ann.

§287.335a	Prohibited activities for pet shop operators.

Minnesota
Minn. Stat. Ann.

§609.52	Theft.

Nevada
Nev. Rev. Stat.

§575.020	Allowing vicious animal to escape or run at large; vicious animal may be killed; liability of person having care or custody of animal which bothers, injures or kills livestock of another.

New Hampshire
N.H. Rev. Stat. Ann.

§471-B:1	Definitions.
§471-B:2	Notice to owner.
§471-B:3	Disposition of abandoned animals.
§471-B:4	Duty of operator.

The world is a big place for a little kitten. If you find a lost kitten, do you own it? Not necessarily.

New Jersey
N.J. Stat. Ann.

§4:19A-1	Program; purpose.
§4:19A-2	Eligibility of owner of dog or cat to participate.
§4:19A-6	Unretrieved animal; final disposition.
§4:21B-1	Establishment and operation to provide services for alteration of reproductive capacity; ordinance; fees.
§4:21B-2	Notarized authorization by owner for consent and agreement to hold harmless.
§4:21B-3	Terms and conditions for maintenance of animal while in custody of clinic.
§4:22-20	Abandoning disabled animal to die in public place; abandoning domesticated animal; disorderly persons offense.
§4:22-26	Acts constituting cruelty in general; penalty.
§4:22-50.1	Arrest of owner or operator of animal pound or shelter for cruelty; petition to remove and appoint receiver; service.

New Mexico
N.M. Stat. Ann.

§77-1-1	Dogs, cats, domesticated fowls and birds are personal property.
§77-1-3	Vaccination of dogs and cats required.
§77-1-4	Vaccination certificates and tags.
§77-1-5	Vaccination of dogs and cats brought into state.
§77-1-6	Notice to health officer of animal bite; confinement.
§77-1-7	Dogs or cats bitten by rabid animals.
§77-1-8	Quarantine.
§77-1-10	Vicious animals; rabid or unvaccinated dogs and cats; procedure following death from rabies.
§77-1-11	Failure to kill; penalty.
§77-1-12	Running at large in municipalities.
§77-1-13	Enforcement.
§77-1-17	Abandoned dogs and cats; notice to owner; disposal without liability.

Your cat gets stuck on a roof. A fireman falls through the roof while rescuing the cat, injuring himself and causing substantial property damage. Who is responsible for the costs? You may have to go to court to get a decision.

New York
N.Y. Agric. & Mkts. Law

§372	Issuance of warrants upon complaint.
§373	Seizure of animals lost, strayed, homeless, abandoned or improperly confined or kept.
§374	Humane destruction or other disposition of animals lost, strayed, homeless, abandoned or improperly confined or kept.
§366	Stealing.
§371	Powers of peace officer.

N.Y. Pub. Health Law

§2803-h	Health related facility; pet therapy programs.

N.Y. Gen. Bus. Law

§741	Definitions.
§742	Sale of animal.
§743	Notice.

N.Y. Envtl. Conserv. Law

§11-0529	Cats hunting birds; or killing other wildlife in certain areas.

N.Y. Lien Law

§183	Lien of bailee of animals.

North Carolina
N.C. Gen. Stat.

§130A-184	Definitions.
§130A-185	Vaccination of all dogs and cats.
§130A-187	County rabies vaccination clinics.
§130A-188	Fee for vaccination at county rabies vaccination clinics.
§130A-189	Rabies vaccination certificates.
§130A-190	Rabies vaccination tags.
§130A-192	Dogs and cats not wearing required rabies vaccination tags.
§130A-193	Vaccination and confinement of dogs and cats brought into N.C.
§130A-194	Quarantine of districts infected with rabies.
§130A-195	Destroying stray dogs and cats in quarantine districts.

§130A-196   Confinement of all biting dogs and cats; notice to local health director; reports by physicians.

§130A-197   Infected dogs and cats to be destroyed; protection of vaccinated dogs and cats.

§130A-198   Confinement.

§130A-199   Rabid animals to be destroyed; heads to be sent to State Laboratory of Public Health.

§130A-200   Confinement or leashing of vicious animals.

Oklahoma
Okla. State. Ann. tit. 4

§501   Disposal of animals kept for pleasure— Method.507 Violation of act as nuisance— Injunction—Abatement.

Oregon
Or. Rev. Stat.

§91.822   Effect of tenant keeping unpermitted pet.

Pennsylvania
Pa. Stat. Ann. tit. 3

§331   Domestic animal defined.

§332   Owner defined.

South Dakota
S.D. Codified Laws Ann.

§7-12-29   Taking and holding animal suspected of being dangerous—Formal determination— Disposal of dangerous animal.

Tennessee
Tenn. Code Ann.

§44-17-113   Bills of sale evidencing purchase of cats or dogs by dealers or research facilities.

§44-17-144   Time dealers must hold cats and dogs after acquisition.

§44-17-115   Authority of commissioner to inspect premises of dealers or research facilities— Inspection of conveyances—Rules and reg-

	ulations regarding inspection.
§44-17-116	Violations of provisions a misdemeanor.

Texas
Tex. Health-Pub. Code Ann.

§3.04	Quarantine of animals.
§3.05	Vaccination of dogs and cats required.
§3.07	Registration of dogs and cats by municipal and county governments.
§3.08	Restraint of dogs and cats of municipal and county governments: Impoundment charges: Disposition of stray animals.
§3.09	Declaration of area quarantine.
§5.03	Violation of dog and cat registration requirements.
§5.04	Violation of dog and cat restraint requirements.
§5.05	Violation of requirement to vaccinate dog or cat.
§5.06	Violation of jurisdictional standards governing the operation of a quarantine or impoundment facility.

Vermont
Vt. Stat. Ann. tit. 13

§420	Vivisection; dogs and cats.
§481	Theft, killing, or injury of domestic animal.

Virginia
Va. Code

§3.1-796.120	Gift, sale, or delivery of animals from pounds or animal shelters.
§3.1-796.122	Cruelty to animals; penalty.
§3.1-796.127	Dogs and cats deemed personal property; rights relating there to.

West Virginia
W.Va. Code

§19-20-9a	Dogs, cats, etc.; rabies observation.
§19-20-12	Dogs, other animals and reptiles protected by law; unlawful killing thereof; aggrieved owner's remedy; penalties; penalties for unlawful stealing of pets.

Wisconsin
Wis. Stat. Ann.

§59.877	Licenses for cats.

Wyoming
Wyo. Stat.

§23-1-101	Definitions of wildlife.

Be sure that your favorite feline wears the proper identification at all times. Doing so may spare you the heartache of a lost cat that is never returned to you.

Index